THE WAY *of* THE MANE

First Edition, 2022

Cover Design: semnitz (99designs)
Interior Layout: Olivier Darbonville

ISBN   979-8-88627-634-3 (print)
979-8-88627-632-9 (ebook)

THE WAY OF THE MANE

ANSWERING THE CALL TO NOBLE MANHOOD BY EMULATING QUALITIES CONSISTENT IN LIONS WITH DARKER MANES

A. T. HOBSON SR.

———

I dedicate this work to my children.

May you ever live to please Christ.

———

CONTENTS

ACKNOWLEDGMENTS

J UNE OF 2016 I RECEIVED ORDERS TO REPORT TO A SMALL base located in South, Korea. Just two months later my wife, our one-year-old daughter, and I were planted in a place called Waegwan, South Korea. Within this small town there stood an old church building that bear an old sign that read "New Testament Christian Church" and it was there within its walls that we discovered two souls that would have an immeasurable impact upon our lives.

With great sincerity of heart I acknowledge my faithful Lord and Savior Jesus Christ Who thought it necessary for my family and I to be swept away to that quiet abode for nearly five years. It was there under the shepherding and example of pastor Fredrick H. Brown Jr. and sister Vera Brown that the Lord began His mighty work in us. This project and the richness of its content has to do with much of what was poured into my life while I and my family were planted abroad. With that said I offer my deepest gratitude to our former pastor and friend for your resilient friendship and dedication to the delicate task of watching for our souls. You both have been our true friends and have demonstrated both the love and heart of Christ before our eyes.

To my wife and dearest friend I thank you for your unending support while this book was in writing. I did not always manage my time properly, but you've been gracious and understanding, nonetheless. It would not have been possible for me to complete this work without my relying on your feedback and much needed spark early on when I just couldn't see it. You've spoken to me words of encouragement during the times that I needed them the most. Thank you for answering the call of God to mother our children making it your daily aim to bring them up in the instruction of the Lord. Your dedication to being our home keeper has established that sure foundation for our children to build upon in times to come. The Lord is using you to preserve the lives of future generations. Great is your reward!

And so it begins...

MY GOAL FOR THIS BOOK IS TO IMPART A HUNGER FOR true righteousness into the hearts of all who commit to journeying with me. In addition, it's my desire that men come to realize their purpose and potential in Christ, and upon this realization, decide to exchange their worldly lives for ones of fruitfulness. It's also my desire that all men bear fruit unto the glory of God, but before we continue further, I think it necessary to clarify what the Scriptures identify as fruit.

There's a common misunderstanding within the religious community where people misidentify what is required to glorify God with our lives. God is not looking for us to accomplish great feats, such as that of crossing the Sahara Desert or climbing the highest mountain, as a means of honoring Him. It's not required or even necessary that we become famous in our field of work or expertise as a way of directing glory to God. We don't have to become successful by the world's standards to bring Him glory. So, what is God looking for? What is necessary for our lives to glorify Him?

Before I answer that, let's consider something. You may recall Christ's conversation with the rich young ruler. Jesus' message to the young man was a simple one: it is difficult for a rich man to enter the Kingdom of God. To this, the

Bible says the disciples, who overheard, were "exceedingly amazed, saying, Who then can be saved?" (Matthew 19:25). Why were they so amazed at the words of Christ concerning the wealthy? It's because they too misunderstood what was necessary to honor God with their lives. They, like many of us, thought that earthly gain equated to godliness. To them, if a person was well off and well established financially, then they were clearly favored by God. This is not always the case. They thought of the religious leaders of that day as being righteous because of the reputation they held with the people, their well put together appearance, and seemingly holy lives. They made themselves appear righteous in the sight of men, but we know that they were far from being righteous in the sight of God. Indeed, Jesus, on numerous occasions, rebuked them for their wicked ways.

So, if accomplishing great acts in the name of religion, obtaining great material success, and merely looking the part doesn't glorify God, what does? It's actually very simple. Contrary to all these things, the Lord simply wants us to produce fruit, because fruit is indicative of life.

In John 15, Jesus identifies Himself as the True Vine and continues to expound upon this very understandable analogy. He says in verse five, "I am the vine, ye are the branches: He that abideth in me, and I in him, the same bringeth forth much fruit." Here we see that it is necessary that we abide in Him if we are to produce the fruit that He speaks of. The spiritual fruit that we produce signals to the world that there is life within us and that life is the very presence of Christ. We are indeed the branches, and just as a branch cannot produce fruit on its own, neither can we apart from Christ.

The Greek translation of fruit is *karpos,* and it means *that which is produced by the inherent energy of a living organism.*[1] It's the stuff you see that traces back to the stuff you don't see. Further, it's the *visible expression of power working inwardly and invisibly.* To put it plainly, the fruit that Jesus desires for us all to possess is the evidence of a life that can easily be traced back to Him as its source of vitality.

So now we have a grasp on what fruit is from a spiritual perspective, but that still doesn't answer the question: How do we glorify God? Jesus tells us plainly in John 15:8, "Herein is my father glorified, that ye bear much fruit; so shall ye be my disciples." This is how we honor the Lord in the sight of all men, by abiding in the vine and producing fruit.

As you journey with me through this book, you will notice that I use both fruit and the mane of a male lion interchangeably. This is because, just as fruit is indicative of the life within a man, so the mane of a male lion reveals his quality. There's a fascinating correlation between the mane of a male lion and the fruit of a man's spirit. The mane has been discovered by zoologists as an accurate assessment of an adult male lion's overall health. It's coloration, denseness, and length tell a story, and reveals a particular lion's fitness, testosterone levels, and eating habits. This open advertisement either attracts onlooking lionesses or pushes them away, dependent upon the quality of his mane. Similarly, dark maned males exercise dominance and superior leadership over males with a softer pigment. Male lions are known by their manes.

In much the same way, men are known by the fruit we possess. It's the part of us that is openly broadcasted to everyone we encounter whether we realize it or not. How we respond to people and situations, how we interact with our wives and children, the manner of our speech, the company we keep, what we find entertaining, the things that pique our interest, our conduct, and hidden life of thought all reveal the fruit of our spirit – whether we're in good health or not. Just as the mane is the first thing you notice when a male lion is approaching, so the fruit within a man is quickly discerned by everyone he encounters. Men are known by the fruit of their spirit – whether ripe or rotten.

Though this aspect of our nature as men is the most important, it's often the part that's overlooked and, in many cases, not even considered. We're living in a time when men monitor their fantasy football league, social media newsfeeds, and their physical looks more than their own spiritual condition. Headphones and air pods occupy the hearing of young men, and its vulgar music they choose over sober thought. They take a greater interest in external pursuits, such as reaching the next promotion and keeping fit in the gym, than in those internal qualities that are of much greater value in the sight of God. There's a great need for fruit in today's American man.

As an active United States servicemember of ten years, I've come to know the culture of my profession very well. Over the years, I've endured the grueling demands of Army life alongside my fellow comrades who have come from all walks of life, from different parts of the country, and from around the world. I've shared tight living quarters over the span of months, slept under the cover of stars, labored in tough conditions, reacted to artillery fire, laughed hysterically, stood honorably, ran repeatedly, and trained religiously with the sons of America. As rewarding as my journey has been up unto this point, I must divulge the truth of the matter: America, our sons are in desperate need of a genuine relationship with God!

In the year 2020, the department of defense processed nearly 8,000 reports of sexual assault, an increase of more than 1,500 from the year prior.[2] Within the last eight years, there have been nearly 50,000 reports of sexual assault within the military, averaging out to about 112 reports a week.[3] These aren't just instances of happenstance. These statistics have an origin and root cause that traces back to a godless culture.

In the same year, the Department of Defense also reported 701 suicides across all military service components.[4] Within the last seven years, there have been 4,366 suicides reported as of December 2020 with the year 2020 being the highest recorded number during that period.[5] That's a lot of fallen soldiers and needless deaths that didn't have to occur. In the past seven years, we've lost more United States servicemembers to suicide than in the war in Iraq that spanned from 2003 to 2010.

There's a lot of men out there that haven't found their purpose in life. We brush shoulders with men every day that have been wounded spiritually and they have no idea of how to heal. These men have yet to find satisfaction in their lives, and so many of them are calling it quits. Maybe you're one of them. If you are, then you've come to the right place. By the end of this book, you will have been challenged in ways you may have never thought possible. Are you ready for this?

Many of these men have never witnessed noble manhood modeled before them, so they've resorted to figuring it out as they go. This is problematic. Boys don't just naturally develop into men of character, and time alone does not incline our hearts toward righteousness. The vine of manhood is one that grows wildly by nature. Unless someone comes along and begins to prune us, providing us with some meaningful criticism and direction, we will only continue to stunt our own growth. Left to ourselves, we become a tangled system incapable of producing our full capacity of fruit.

Bear in mind that the military is just a sample of America's overall population. It's a melting pot of different people from different parts of the country that accurately represents what we look like as a whole. These numbers are a cry for help from men all over our nation! *The Way of the Mane* is an answer to those cries.

This book is a call for men to awaken to the state of our spiritual condition and, upon this awakening, seek to develop fruit within our lives unto the glory of God. By the end of this book, you will agree with me that every man bears a mane and that the greatest feat we can attempt to accomplish in pursuit of the glory of God is to set out unhesitatingly along *The Way of the Mane.*

One

The Way of the Mane

THE SERENGETI LION PROJECT IS A CONTINUOUS FIELD study of lions in their natural environment and is an initiative that's been ongoing for over 45 years. Much of what we know about lions today has derived from data collected from this project. They explore questions such as why lions live in prides in comparison to their big-cat counterparts who primarily lead solitary lives, how lions choose their habitat, how moonlight plays a part in a pride's decision to hunt, and why lions choose their mates. These and so many other questions have all been answered through numerous field studies over the years. A lot of hard work, money, time, and resources have gone into educating the world on the African lion.

Craig Packer, the man in charge, has spent a great deal of time in Africa studying the lion. In his decades of research, he and his team have unraveled the many mysteries of lion culture, but what strikes me the most is his discovery of the purpose behind the lion mane.

Undoubtedly, it's one of the most iconic features of any creature to ever walk the earth. It ranks above the ivory tusks of elephants, the fashionable print of cheetahs, and even the brazen bottoms of baboons. Like a genetic crown placed by God Himself, the mane represents power, strength, and head-level authority. It's the easiest way to positively identify a male lion; he's known by his mane.

Young males gradually develop their own budding manes, thus resembling princes still under the tutelage of their kingly fathers. Their scruffy beards foretell the story of future rulership. Time and experience will ensure they wear it rightfully. Without his mane, the male lion wouldn't be as ferocious, as formidable, as feared as he is today.

We Are Known by Our Manes

Packer and his field staff hired a toy company to create two life-sized lions to use for their next study. They were curious to discover how both lions and lionesses might respond to lions with manes differing in color. Does the shade of the mane matter? Does it play a part in a lioness's decision in choosing a mate? Does it communicate a message to other males, and if so, what exactly is that message?

To relieve this curiosity, they had the life-sized, stuffed lions shipped to their field site in the Serengeti National Park in Tanzania where they attached mane samples to their necks. Each stuffed lion wore a different colored mane. One was blond and one black. Both were placed in a small clearing accompanied by a speaker. After some time, they observed a lioness approaching the dummy's position. She moved slowly but steadily toward the sound of hyenas squabbling over a kill that was playing from the speaker. When she noticed the dummies, the crew turned the speaker off and remained dead silent, waiting to see which stuffed lion she would show an interest in. She chose the dark-maned dummy. She sniffed under the dummy's tail and then laid directly in front of him to communicate that she had chosen him.

The team concluded that lionesses are most attracted to lions with darker manes, since two other females did the exact same thing, showing no regard for the blond-maned male. It turned out that the mane did in fact matter in terms of attracting the opposite sex. But what does this mean for other males? Does the shade of a male lion's mane play a social role in exerting dominance over other males? Packer and his team discovered the answer to be yes.

The same experiment was staged again, except this time, a band of two adult male lions were enticed to approach the dummies. The crew played the sound of a roaring lioness over the loudspeaker that drew the attention of the males. Packer recalls the scene in his book, *Lions in the Balance:*

> "And here they come, one of these boys has a darker mane than the other, and as often happens, the dark-maned male leads the way. They can see the dummies, and their approach is slow, deliberate; caution is written all over their faces. Forty meters, then twenty, and finally, at ten meters, their choice is clear... The dark-maned male sniffs beneath the tail of the blond-maned dummy; his companion joins the investigation."[6]

The team concluded that dark-maned males attracted females but were intimidating to other rival males.

As I stated before, lions are known by their manes, primarily because the mane, as Packer puts it, "is an honest advertisement of a male's overall health; every male has a genetic predisposition to grow a mane – and mane hair continues to grow as long as the male maintains reasonably good health. But only the best can produce enough testosterone to grow a black mane."[7] Studies have shown that males with darker manes have higher levels of testosterone, which is a deterrent to contending males but an attraction for females. More testosterone means security in the mind of a lioness. A darker mane signifies a stronger mate. The lionesses choose their mates based on the male lion's potential to lead them and their future cubs. Studies have also shown that dark-maned males survive longer when wounded in a fight, and that their cubs are more likely to reach maturity.

Because the color of the mane is dependent upon the health of the lion, his dieting plays a key factor in its coloration. This means if a lion started out as a blond, some good consistent dieting could help him develop into a black-maned male. We'll discuss this further in chapter two, "Selective Eating."

Either make the tree good, and his fruit good; or else make the tree corrupt, and his fruit corrupt: for the tree is known by his fruit.

MATTHEW 12:33

Jesus said the above verse in response to an accusation the Pharisees made against Him. In their envy, they accused Him of casting out devils by the power of Satan, no doubt attempting to discredit Jesus' power and sway the opinion of the people that stood by. But Jesus revealed to them and to us a very simple principle, and it's this: *Men are known by their fruit.*

Even as the mane is indicative of a lion's state of health, so the fruit of a man's spirit is a snapshot of his spiritual fitness.

What we produce day-in and day-out hangs visibly before the eyes of all men; we are known by our fruit. The spiritual food we intake every day is manifested to everyone by our lives; we are known by our manes. This is the premise for this entire book. The fact that men are known and recognized by something much deeper than the clothes we wear, the cars we drive, or the careers we choose is insightful. These things all add to our physical image – how people view us external- ly. Most men put their stock in these things because they're concerned with the things of the flesh. One hundred percent of their time, energy, and thought goes into bettering how they are viewed externally, while no energy or consideration is given to the hidden life within. They possess what Scripture refers to as a carnal mind, and this is one of the reasons we must have our minds renewed by the washing of God's Word.

For they that are after the flesh do mind the things of the flesh; but they that are after the Spirit the things of the Spirit.

ROMANS 8:5

As followers of Christ, we are no longer concerned with the things of the flesh. Through our faith in Him and the revela- tion of His Word, we've gained the enlightenment of a much nobler and much higher way of life. Now we follow the way of the Spirit, hence *The Way of the Mane*. Intangible qualities, such as love, joy, peace, longsuffering, gentleness, goodness, faith, meekness, and temperance, can only be adopted through the indwelling of God's Spirit. These all add to our spiritual image – how people perceive us spiritually. This is of much greater importance than how we may be known physically.

Spillage

I left the office early one day in an attempt to beat traffic into the city and stopped by the house to pick up my wife and kids before getting on the road. It was our pastor's 50th birthday, so we were leaving to purchase his gift. While in route, my daughter had complained once or twice about being hungry. We didn't have any food in the car except for a banana. I thought to give it to her, but when I picked it up, I could see that it was no good. The outward peeling was almost totally brown in color, and there was some liquid leaking from it. It was entirely spoiled. I came to this conclusion, not because the outside was brown, but because the fruit within was soft, mushy, and leaking from the inside out. The rottenness of the inward fruit had manifested itself outwardly! It was quite clear that had I given my daughter this banana, her tummy wouldn't have agreed with it.

It's not hard to spot bad fruit. If you've ever been to the produce section of any grocery store, you'd have no problem agreeing with me. All it takes is a few seconds of casually comparing apples or oranges for us to decipher the bad from the good. In fact, we'll pick up several different apples before we decide on the one we want. If it's too soft, that's an indicator of bad fruit. If it has holes in it, that's an indicator of bad fruit. If it's browning on the outside and losing its color, that's an indicator of bad fruit. We wouldn't dare spend our hard-earned money on bad fruit when we can simply reach for something a bit fresher, something of better quality.

In like manner, every man possesses fruit. It's an element of our being that is constantly being broadcasted to everyone around us. Fruit is to man as mane is to lion. Just as God gave us the ability to decipher between good and bad fruit, so too He gives us indicators that assist us in determining the fruit within ourselves and others. The content of our speech is an indicator. How we interact and respond to others are indicators. How we treat our children and our wives are indicators. How we respond to life's challenges, setbacks, failures, successes, and pressures are all indicators, and the list can go on and on. The point is that God has given every man the ability to differentiate between good and bad fruit, by simply observing the life lived.

As I stated earlier, what we produce day-in and day-out hangs visibly before the eyes of all men; we are known by our fruit. The spiritual food we intake every day is manifested to everyone by our lives; we are known by our manes. Knowing this will help us in determining our fruitfulness – whether we're bearers of the good or the corrupt.

The Sixth Sense

It had been over three years since Peter had forsaken his fisherman's boat and set out to follow a Man he didn't know. Throughout that period, he witnessed inexplicable wonders on a daily basis as he walked alongside the King of the universe. His eyes beheld sights that would rock our world and completely turn it upside down. He saw things that would challenge any man's understanding of life. But Peter wasn't just a witness to these miracles; he was also the subject of some of them.

Peter didn't have even the faintest idea about what he would experience when he decided to forsake his nets and follow Jesus. There's no way he could have anticipated such phenomena. Peter never dreamed of stepping out of a boat and walking firmly upon troubled waters, but he did. He couldn't have imagined what it would be like seeing angels ascend and descend upon the Son of God, but he saw them. His heart tried to grasp all the wonder every time his eyes caught the power of God.

Three years had transpired, and now Peter was carrying the torch the Lord had lit and passed on to him before His ascension. But his following of the Christ began with a sixth sense. Peter would have never left his boat had he not sensed that he needed to. He would have been like many men today who live mediocre lives: fishing for fish when they can be fishing for men!

There was something about Jesus that called out to him, reaching him personally and inspiring him to forsake all that he had ever known. Jesus possessed something within Himself that drew Peter. There were qualities about Him that convinced Peter that forsaking all would be worth it, and those qualities were none other than the fruit of the Spirit of God. When the Spirit of God is leading the way, others are sure to follow.

When you've purposed to bear fruit in your life, it won't be long before other men flock to your tree. They'll take an interest in you, wondering what makes you so different. Periodically, they'll approach you, asking for advice or your opinion on certain matters that they find challenging. When they look at you, you'll notice a sense of reverence coupled with an underlining desire to emulate your character. Remember, it's not you they're admiring, but it's the Spirit of God inside of you. It's the fruit that's so vividly hanging before their eyes. It's the darkness of the mane around your spiritual neck.

Peter immediately discerned fruit within Jesus, and this is what moved him to forsake everything and everyone to follow Him. Perhaps it was the fruit of love that was radiating off Him that drew Peter to such a life-changing decision. He discerned that the Spirit of God was upon Him, and He wanted to be where the Spirit was, and that's the sixth sense: discernment.

Discernment is the ability to detect with the eyes. As Christian men, it's vital we understand and apply this sixth sense if we're to lead fruitful lives and bear manes that grow darker with time. We'll need to detect every area within our lives that's lacking fruit. If we desire others to follow us as we follow Christ, we will need to ensure that we are in fact following Christ. An easy way to assess whether we're walking along *The Way* is to examine our fruitfulness. Take the time to ask yourself these three questions and really consider your answer:

1. If my actions in life were to be represented by apples, would I be a tree that bears good or spoiled fruit?

2. Does my mane validate my ability to lead my family and others, or does it only reveal that I'm straddling the fence of Christianity?

3. When others see me, what exactly do they see?

These are good questions that will aid us in determining the state of our fruitfulness. To help you gauge where you stand, below is a basket of fruit taken from Galatians 5:22. As you read the list below, assess on a scale of 1 to 10 where you stand with each quality. Try and visualize the condition of each quality in your life as an apple or banana and whether it would appear fresh or foul. Consider how others, those closest to you, would assess each quality in your life as well:

Self-Assessment

Rate yourself on a scale of zero to ten on how often you embody the fruit of the Spirit, with zero being the complete absence of that particular fruit in your day-to-day life and ten representing a constant flow.

Love – How often do you demonstrate unconditional love toward others?

0 1 2 3 4 5 6 7 8 9 10

Joy – How often do you exemplify the joy of the Lord?

0 1 2 3 4 5 6 7 8 9 10

Peace – How often is your mind settled upon quietly trusting in the Lord?

0 1 2 3 4 5 6 7 8 9 10

Longsuffering – How often do you overlook the offences of others?

0 1 2 3 4 5 6 7 8 9 10

Gentleness – How often are you genuinely kind toward others?

0 1 2 3 4 5 6 7 8 9 10

Goodness – How inclined are you to desire good things for others?

0 1 2 3 4 5 6 7 8 9 10

Faith – How well does your life reflect that you trust in God?

0 1 2 3 4 5 6 7 8 9 10

Meekness – How well does the conduct of your life reflect submissiveness to God?

0 1 2 3 4 5 6 7 8 9 10

Temperance – How likely are you to control your temper in a moment of anger or frustration?

0 1 2 3 4 5 6 7 8 9 10

Remember when I mentioned that there are indicators that reveal bad fruit such as discoloration, softness, spillage, and so on? Well, the qualities above are all indicators of the complete opposite. They reveal to us and others our level of fruitfulness. They reveal the state of our manes. Developing the qualities above is what we should strive for each day, because in doing so, we commit to living within the pleasure of Almighty God.

Spoiled, Rotten, and Absolutely No Good

Fruit is attractive. It draws the eye. It incites the appetite. It awakens our cravings and lures the hungry. It's what our children want more than their veggies. It's what we need in place of candy. It's sweet and sometimes sour in a good way. It tastes good and keeps us wanting more. All of this is true when fruit is good – when it's ripe and ready. But if we were to describe fruit after it has lost its ripeness, we would have a completely different description.

It stinks. It's not attractive. It kills our appetite. It'll make us sick if we partake of it. We detest it. We throw it in the garbage. We get rid of it as quickly as we can and even avoid touching it in the process. Simply put, we don't like bad fruit and neither does God.

Beware lest any man spoil you through philosophy and vain deceit, after the tradition of men, after the rudiments of the world, and not after Christ.

COLOSSIANS 2:8

Spoil. That's the word the Apostle Paul chose to describe what happens to men who foolishly and passively follow the teachings, traditions, and ways of this present world. A literal internal decaying begins when we choose either ignorantly or passively to adhere to the teachings, traditions, and ways of the world. Rotten character is preserved for those who follow the crowd as opposed to following Christ, and this is the problem our families, communities, and nation are faced with today. We live in a time where an overwhelming majority of men, young and old, are producing spoiled fruit primarily due to corrupt influences.

Physical presence is no longer the primary means of influencing others as it once was. More and more, men are utilizing social and mainstream media to keep relevance in the minds of men like you and I. Music is often innocently portrayed as a means of creative expression, but it doesn't take twenty-twenty vision to see that music is being used as an avenue for ungodly propaganda. Men who don't possess a genuine love for Jesus are using this and many other mediums to spread a message completely contrary to our Father's Word.

Men have been deceived into believing the ways of the world are more relevant than God's ways and His Word as a result of adhering to these indirect influences. Scripture tells us in 1 Corinthians 15:33, "Be not deceived: evil communications corrupt good manners." In layman's terms, bad company always produces bad fruit. Exercising our sixth sense couldn't be more necessary than in this present time that we're living in. We must pay attention to the men we surround ourselves with both directly and indirectly. We must ask ourselves questions like:

1. What is this guy all about?

2. What direction is he heading in from a biblical perspective?

3. Does he genuinely love the Lord or does he only appear to?

4. What sort of fruit does he possess?

5. If he had a mane, what shade would it be?

Paul cautions us in saying, "Beware lest any man..." It doesn't matter their social status or educational level, whether they're successful in business or politics or what their level of fame may be. Paul says, "any man," and I'm glad he didn't specify a particular group. Keeping it broad helps us to remember that all men are fallen from glory, and caution should be exercised when entrusting any man with our time and undivided attention.

I came across a video of a man passionately sharing a message that seemed to be positive – the key word being "seemed." He spoke about the need for people to seek clarity in their lives. In his words, "Too many people are skating on the surface of life," and the fix, according to him, was to seek clarity in four major areas of your life. He's a New York Times bestselling author and has a great following. He seems to have it all together. He's successful by the world's standards and seems to be happy with his life. We should listen to him, right? Wrong! In all his talk and emphasis about seeking clarity, he never once mentioned the need for people to come to Christ as the only means of obtaining that clarity. He never pinpointed Christ as the only means through which we all can find clarity in our lives, and in fact, he never mentioned Christ at all! That's a problem!

That's a big problem!

His message is received by many people, including professing Christians, because many lack clarity about who they are, and their sixth sense is too dull to decipher between bad and good fruit. Look at what Paul has to say about men like this, men who preach and teach doctrines other than that of Christ:

But though we, or an angel from heaven, preach any other gospel unto you than that ye have received, let him be accursed. As we said before, so say I now again, if any man preach any other gospel unto you than that ye have received, let him be accursed.

GALATIANS 1:8-9

Did you see what Paul said in the latter part of the second verse? He said, "If any man," just as he said before in Colossians 2:8. If we're to lead others to Christ, we will need to know how to decipher between the bad and the good. We will need to choose wisely the men we follow and associate with because, remember, bad company always produces bad fruit.

Jesus was adamant about teaching this same principle and ensured His disciples understood the importance of disassociating with men who possessed bad fruit, particularly the Scribes, Pharisees, and Sadducees. These three groups were viewed by the public as blessed men of God primarily because they maintained positions of authority within the religious community and always presented themselves in the finest raiment. But Jesus saw them for who they were. He saw beyond their external front and marked them as men of spoiled, rotten, and absolutely no good fruit.

They were thought to have favor from God because of their physical reputation and earthly success, but the favor of God was certainly not with them. On the contrary, they were the primary group Jesus found fault in. Consider this strong reproof given by Jesus:

Woe unto you, scribes and Pharisees, hypocrites! For ye are like unto whited sepulchers, which indeed appear beautiful outward, but are within full of dead men's bones, and of all uncleanness. Even so ye also outwardly appear righteous unto men, but within ye are full of hypocrisy and iniquity.

MATTHEW 23:27-28

Jesus' sixth sense was sharp to the touch. Using His two-edged sword – the Word – He was always able to cut away and see beyond the outward appearance of man, looking deeper into the thoughts and intentions of the heart (Hebrews 4:12). The Word of God is always what Jesus used as the principle authority and reason for His judgement calls. God's Word in the hearts and minds of His people is what enables us to develop our sixth sense of discernment. Without it, our minds are carnal and spiritually dull, incapable of seeing beyond the outward appearance. This is important to note, because if we're to accurately assess our level of fruitfulness and gain a greater understanding of the state of our manes, we will have to rely upon the Word of God. God's Word is what we measure ourselves up against when seeking the truth about ourselves. His Word is a clear reflection of His Person – Jesus, the man we all must emulate. The Prophet Isaiah's response upon seeing the Lord high and lifted up drives this point home:

---

*Then said I, Woe is me! for I am undone; because I am a man of
unclean lips, and I dwell in the midst of a people of unclean lips:
for mine eyes have seen the King, the Lord of hosts.*

ISAIAH 6:5

Isaiah was able to see the error of His ways once He saw the Lord! The presence of God revealed to him where he was falling short. God's holiness shed light upon his unholiness. Thus, the Word of God helps us to see our blemishes that are often hidden and tucked away deep within the innerworkings of our hearts. Jesus said in John 15:22, "If I had not come and spoken unto them, they had not had sin: but now they have no cloak for their sin." The Word incarnate exposed the hidden sin of man, and the written Word does the same today.

As we journey together through these pages, I challenge you to allow God's Word and His messages that are woven throughout to speak to your inner man. Be receptive to what the Spirit of God is saying and pray that the Lord helps you to see the truest state of your mane. If it turns out that you discover you're spiritually malnourished, take heart and know that such a discovery is the initial step in bearing good fruit. We must know where we are before we can possibly know where we are going.

Two

Selective Eater

*Man shall not live by bread alone, but by every word that
proceedeth out of the mouth of God.*

MATTHEW 4:4

MY WIFE AND I MADE IT A POINT TO BEFRIEND ANOTH-er couple that was new to our church. After Sunday
morning service we invited them to lunch at a local restau-
rant which happened to be my favorite in town. Once we
arrived, we each sat down, and a menu was brought to our
table. In South Korea, one menu is given to each table as opposed to the American standard, where each diner receives
their own. I had been to the restaurant enough times to know
what I wanted without looking over the menu. It was the
shrimp fried rice that brought me back every time. I raved
about this restaurant and dish to anyone who asked of me a
good place to eat locally. While we're on the topic, if you ever
find yourself in Waegwan, South Korea, look for a restaurant
named I Am Cook. Once you arrive, ask for menu item number 26, and maybe you'll agree.

So, there we were, sitting, talking, and helping them navigate the menu. Being that it was his first time at the restaurant, he asked if I had any recommendations, and as expected, I recommended menu item number 26, the shrimp fried rice. All the while, I was thinking, "He's really going to enjoy this meal," but I never expected what came next.

Our dishes were brought to the table and placed in front of us. We blessed the food collectively, and I immediately dove in. The dish was as good as I had remembered, hot and fresh fried rice with shrimp, diced egg, and mushrooms with a semi sweet sauce added as a dressing. My plate was almost clean when something struck me. I noticed that my new friend wasn't eating. He was noticeably skeptical about the contents of his plate. As he, with chopsticks maneuvered pieces of mushroom into a secluded corner of his plate, I could see that he didn't have any interest in eating the dish. It became clear to me that my new friend was a selective eater.

Most men take greater precaution in the food they eat than in the music they listen to, the content they watch via social media, or in cinema. While dieting is important from a physical standpoint, it's of even greater importance spiritually. What we regularly feed our inner man will determine the state of our manes, whether we're capable of producing a full dark mane that shows forth spiritual power and strength.

A Cause for Wariness

God very clearly, through His Word, instructs us to be wary of many things. Exercising caution is wise because it protects us from potential harm. For example, we teach our children to look both ways before crossing the street, because of the potential danger involved in getting to the other side.

We carefully consider the location of our homes, because we want to provide the best educational opportunities for our children and ensure our families are safe from harm. From our choice of friends to the restaurants we dine in or the areas of town we stay away from, we're constantly exercising caution. Whether we realize it or not, we keep a roll of mental caution tape with us everywhere we go, so it should be no surprise to us when God instructs us to beware of certain people, places, and things.

Beware lest any man spoil you through philosophy and vain deceit, after the tradition of men, after the rudiments of the world, and not after Christ.

COLOSSIANS 2:8

I referenced the above scripture in the first chapter as well, because I can't express enough the importance of ensuring we're following Jesus and not the world.

Beware! That's a strong word, isn't it? When I hear this word, an image of a red sign posted on the gate of someone's backyard immediately comes to mind. I think of King, my grandfather's full bred and well-fed German Shepherd. I think of when King almost tore me to pieces. If the word beware should have been posted on any gate in the world it should have been posted on his gate.

I was home on leave with my wife visiting my grandmother, and I was excited to take King for a walk around the block. My grandfather had passed away a few years back, and I thought for sure King would be happy to see me. German Shepherds are as loyal as you can imagine, so in my mind, I thought King would recognize that I was a part of the family. I used to cut the grass in King's cage, so I thought for sure he'd recognize his old friend. I was wrong. King and I hadn't had enough face time, and by the time of my visit, he was fully grown.

I opened the top hatch to King's cage and snapped the leash. He couldn't contain himself as I opened the gate to let him out. My right forearm flexed immediately as I struggled to gain control of him. I tightened my grip on the leash, but it didn't matter. He was pulling me the whole way around. By the time we made it back to my grandmother's side of the block, my grandmother stood at the end of the driveway facing the street King and I were walking on. King saw her, but just as soon as he did, I turned him about and proceeded to go for a run. Bad move! Without hesitation he began gnawing at my feet and growling in displeasure. Before I knew it, he had knocked me down, planted his paws on my chest, and viciously growled in my face, showing me all of his canines. My heart melted as I quickly tried to prepare for what he might do next. My instinctive response was to lock eyes with him. I did as I grabbed his collar with both hands, assertively shouting, "King! King! It's me! Get down!"

By the grace of God, he lost interest, dropped down from my chest and permitted me to walk him to his cage. I unlatched the leash and closed the hatch. My life was spared. Claw marks left on the front of my right forearm serve as a life-long reminder of what it means to beware.

In essence, when we hear "beware," we think of potential danger. But whoever thought such danger could come in the form of mere words flowing from the mouth of another person? Have you ever considered teachings or traditions as dangerous? I mean, danger is accidentally falling into a lion's den. Danger is stumbling upon an armed robbery taking place at your local convenience store. Danger is swimming in shark infested waters, right? If we're talking from an earthly perspective, then yes, that is danger to beware of. But this book seeks to teach the way of the Spirit, so in terms of spiritual danger, words present great hazard to any man's life. Teachings and traditions that are not biblically based are dangerous to the Christian man. Multiple times throughout the gospels, we witness Jesus charging His disciples to beware of certain people, places, and things. Here's a list of a few:

Of False Prophets

Beware of false prophets, which come to you in sheep's clothing, but inwardly they are ravening wolves.

Matthew 7:15

Of Men

But beware of men: for they will deliver you up to the councils, and they will scourge you in their synagogues.

Matthew 10:17

Of the Doctrine of Men

Then Jesus said unto them, take heed and beware of the leaven of the Pharisees and of the Sadducees.

Matthew 16:6

Of Covetousness

And he said unto them, take heed, and beware of covetousness: for a man's life consisteth not in the abundance of things which he possesseth.

Luke 12: 15

Of What You Hear

And he said unto them, take heed what ye hear: with what measure ye mete, it shall be measured to you: and unto you that hear shall more be given.

Mark 4:24

Jesus thinks it's important that we use caution if we're going to follow Him. We will have to be alert and aware of our surroundings every moment of every day, taking extra precaution with what we hear because words are what we live by.

A Limitless Capacity

If you're intent on being a lion that shows forth a full black mane, which as we've learned is indicative of a healthy and spiritually fruitful life, then you will want to closely monitor your food intake; you will want to be a selective eater.

But he answered and said, It is written, Man shall not live by bread alone, but by every word that proceedeth out of the mouth of God.

MATTHEW 4:4

As you may well know, lions are carnivores which means they eat meat – and lots of it. An average adult male lion can consume up to 60 pounds of meat in one sitting. However, they require about 10 to 15 pounds per day for survival. Because they require so much meat every day, lions are known for being opportunistic. They're constantly driven to consume. It's how they're physically wired. They will eat mostly anything they can put their paws on with the exception of rotten meat. Some lions won't stoop so low as to endure the smell of a highly spoiled carcass, regardless of how hungry they may be. While some lions, dependent upon their environment, prey availability, and other factors, will scavenge for food, lions primarily prefer to hunt their own prey. Unlike scavengers, they require a certain standard in dieting and it's a simple one: partake of only what is pure.

Scavengers such as vultures or hyenas have a greater threshold or tolerance for rotten meat than other animals. A hyena can maintain a diet consisting only of foul meat and continue in its health. They can literally eat anything to include the bone of their prey and meat that's been decaying for weeks. It's how they're physically wired. Lions, on the other hand, have a low tolerance for rotten meat in comparison to scavengers.

The words of the Lord are pure: as silver tried in a furnace of earth, purified seven times.

PSALM 12:6

As Christian men, our only source of spiritual meat is the Word of God. The Words of our Father are literally what we live by as new creatures in Christ. Remember, Jesus said, "Man shall not live by bread alone, but by every word that proceedeth out of the mouth of God" (Matthew 4:4). As men, naturally we'd be hard pressed to down 60 pounds of meat in a month, let alone one sitting! But our inner man has a feeding capacity greater than that of the natural man. He hungers after more and more of whatever we feed him. Our spiritual bellies have a limitless capacity. There's a man deep within every man that possesses an intense craving for the Words of God. There is nothing else that will satisfy his hunger. The man on the inside yearns for the pure meat of God's Word and suffers from the pains of starvation the more we neglect it. We must purpose to feed on the Word of God and satisfy the hunger of the man inside.

Our tolerance for spoiled meat, such as vulgarity, perverseness, injustice, foul language and behavior, lustfulness, and all ungodliness, dramatically decreases the more we get to know God through His Word. The more we eat His Word the more we crave It, and the less we find interest in spoiled meat. His Word should be what we purpose to feed our inner-man every day because His Words are pure. Remember, words are what we live by as new creations in Christ, and though you may not become what you eat, you will be affected by it, which is all the more reason to be a selective eater.

Imagine being a lion with a digestive system accustomed to processing large volumes of meat daily. Now consider the physical torment and absolute agony you would go through had you wandered the open plains for a week with no success of finding anything besides spoiled meat. You'd either starve or die of sickness. Many times, men go days, weeks, and even months without ever reading and meditating upon a passage of scripture. This willful neglect of God's Word will always cause us to starve spiritually, and over time, it'll create blemishes in our mane rendering us unusable by God.

Look at how Jim George, the author of *A Man After God's Own Heart,* explains his hunger experience: "I am among those who, when I was young, went to church regularly, but that was it... I came to my senses at about age 30 and realized I was starving to death spiritually."[8] It's unfortunate he had to wait until he was 30 to begin experiencing the satisfying effect of God's Word. You may think, "But 30 is still young." This is true, but what of the 15 plus years he spent starving his inner man? He'd be a more refined and stronger man had he begun to walk with the Lord earlier. Don't wait until you're "of age" to begin walking with God. There is no better time than now because we can't even be sure we'll see tomorrow. It's best to serve the Lord as soon as you hear His call.

If we don't have a desire for God's Word, then it should cause us to examine why:

- What have I prioritized above time in God's Word?

- What have I been eating lately that's replaced my hunger for purity?

- Am I a selective eater or do I feast on whatever is available?

We should never get used to eating anything other than God's Word, because there can be no supplement for His Word. Nothing else is capable of providing what It provides. Nothing else is capable of revealing what It reveals. Nothing else is capable of satisfying our spiritual hunger.

Going several days without opening the Bible and spending time in His Word is just unacceptable for a Christian man. When you have a limitless capacity for consumption, a constant flow of substance is needed to sustain you, because what you consume is constantly being burned. It's simple physics. Continual output requires continual input. On the other hand, minimal output requires minimal input. If you're someone who others rely on for encouragement or emotional support, you require a continual flow of encouragement and emotional support yourself. You can't give what you don't have. When we attempt to do this, it always manifests itself in frustration and impatience. God's Word provides us the strength we need to be strong for others.

We should desire the meat of His Word so much that going a day without reading It should pain us. Going a day without meditating on It should remind us of the intense suffering we're putting the man on the inside through. But your sensitivity to your internal need for the substance of Scripture is dependent upon the depth of your relationship with Him. When you've grown accustomed to being in the presence of the Lord, and when the sweetness of His Spirit within you has been your daily experience, a day without seeking Him will pain your soul. But if you haven't been walking with Him and seeking Him hasn't been your daily devotion, your sensitivity toward the necessity of His Word will not be as keen. If we have a shallow relationship with God, which really is no relationship at all, our tolerance level for sin will be greater. We, like scavengers, will grow accustomed to a foul diet. However, if we purpose to feed our inner man with His Word and prioritize His will above all else, our threshold drops dramatically. We begin to desire purity when we've tasted of purity.

Location Is Everything

Up until now, I've talked a great deal about spiritual fruit and our need to develop more in our lives. I've also highlighted a connection between the mane of a lion and the quality or fruit of our spirits. Fruit and manes go hand in hand and believe it or not lions and trees have a lot in common. For one, they're both capable of producing something that attracts others. Trees produce fruit that draw the hungry, and lions grow manes that attract lionesses and invokes a desire for weaker males to follow them. Another commonality shared between the two is that they both greatly rely upon location for survival. If this were the land of Oz and you were able to have a conversation with a tree and ask it where it would like to settle down for retirement, it would respond with something like, "Somewhere by the water." What's interesting is if you asked a lion that same question, his response would be the same.

Blessed is the man that walketh not in the council of the ungodly, nor standeth in the way of sinners, not sitteth in the seat of the scornful. But his delight is in the law of the Lord; and in his law doth he meditate day and night. And he shall be like a tree planted by the rivers of water, that bringeth forth his fruit in his season; his leaf shall not wither; and whatsoever he doeth shall prosper.

PSALM 1:1-3

Trees thrive in areas where there is plenty of water. Rivers provide the best location for them to maintain their water supply. The blessed man spoken of in Psalm 1 is likened unto a tree planted by rivers of water. He knows where his supply comes from and purposes to always ensure he's in the right location. Notice where he doesn't walk, stand, or sit. He plants himself by the river. His roots are able to draw from the river which is why his leaf never withers away. He has a continual supply of water in all seasons of his life.

In the last day, that great day of the feast, Jesus stood and cried, saying, If any man thirst, let him come unto me, and drink. He that believeth on me, as the scripture hath said, out of his belly shall flow rivers of living water. (But this spake he of the Spirit, which they that believe on him should receive...)

JOHN 7:37-39

God's Holy Spirit is the perpetual water supply that every Christian man needs if we're to produce fruit. Sometimes, it's best to just look around when determining what sort of man you are. Our location, where we choose to spend the majority of our time, will tell on us. If we delight in the ways of the world as opposed to the ways of God, we willingly remove ourselves from our supply and thereby forfeit our potential for producing good fruit. Location is everything. Whether we become good or corrupt trees will always point back to where we're planted.

Lions thrive when they're able to secure territory by a major confluence. They use the land area where two rivers meet as a funnel for thirsty prey. They know that the river draws much prey, and so, when deciding where to occupy territory, wise lions migrate to major confluences. Considering that a confluence has a river on either side, there's an abundant supply of vegetation. This means there's plenty of places to use for cover, which is great news for lions. Again, location is everything, and if you're intent on leading a healthy life that enables you to produce a full black mane, you'll want to make the river your friend. We'll discuss this more in chapter four, "The Hopcraft Effect."

Three

Men of Risk (MOR)

Why sit we here until we die?

2 KINGS 7:3

IT'S ONE HUNDRED AND TEN DEGREES AND NOT A SINGLE cloud is in sight as you prowl the open plains, desperately looking for something that will feed you and your pride of lions. It's been eight days since your last kill, and you are again forced into survival mode. It never ends. All you've known is high and low for as long as you can remember, and today you find yourself experiencing the burdens of desperation again. You continue to search hungrily as you carry the weight of your 400-pound frame. Each step becomes increasingly wearisome.

You've lost an alarming amount of energy and now your reserves are kicking in. You know that time is of the essence. You can sense that you've just literally stepped into a life-or-death predicament, and if you continue without substance, you will eventually collapse in exhaustion. Everything is keen. Everything is heavy now. Even the weight of your mane has become irritably noticeable.

Everyone is tired. Fatigue is written all over your pride's movements. Your young ones struggle to keep up. They need shade. They need a break from the trek. They need just a moment of rest, but their overarching need for meat discourages you from giving them leave to rest. You have to continue forward because, at this point, a pause would mean death.

As you turn about to assess everyone's condition, you can see through the haze of the day that they're all on the verge of starvation. They're all wanting to just quit. They're almost completely persuaded to simply give in, but something keeps them moving forward. Something causes them to grit their teeth and grind onward. That something is their trust in your ability to lead them. Your presence alone encourages them to bear a little longer, to go a little further. They keep telling themselves, "He knows the way!"

But your mane is paling as a result of an inconsistent diet. You've been out on the plains away from the confluence for far too long and your inconsistency substance has caused your mane to fade from black. But you're the only mane-bearer the pride has. Your semi dark mane juxtaposed against the tall yellow grass acts as their guide. When you stop, they stop. When you crouch, they crouch. If you even for a second show a sign of defeat, they'll...no! You have to keep their hope alive! You have to project confidence. They need you. They're following your every move.

Just when all hope seems to be lost, you catch the sound of a herd of buffalo just meters beyond your position. You can hear them lowing in the near distance. Your heart rate rises. Blood begins to surge through your veins as the excitement of a hunt begins to energize your muscles. Your pride has caught the sudden shift of momentum, and their posture changes from soaked leaves to oak branches. They're alive again! They're ready for anything! Their volume meter just jumped from zero to one hundred, and they're ready to risk it all for a shot at some prime rib.

Still, they're mindful to follow your lead. As hungry as they may feel and as desperate as they may be, they respect your mane enough to trust your timing. Your mane symbolizes experience in their eyes, and considering the shade of it, having still streaks of black, your record of victory stretches long and wide. They hold steady.

You're moving as a single unit. Everyone is on high alert. The pains of starvation are temporarily silenced by the thought of the rewards that lie ahead. You approach the crown of a hill attempting to gain a greater vantage point, and there they are, at least three hundred cape buffalo spread across the open plain. All you need is one to ensure your pride's survival. One buffalo will feed you and yours for many days, but you know from experience the kill won't come easy. You even begin to doubt whether you possess the energy necessary to take on such a challenge. But if not you, then who?

The females of the pride are excellent hunters, but these are not antelope; we're talking anywhere from 900 to 1900 pounds of massive beast. That's the equivalent of nearly 20 tracks of the New York City subway system. That's weight! That's heavy! A lioness wouldn't stand a chance.

This is nothing like your standard ambush scenario. You won't be able to hide in the brush and surprise this sort of prey. He won't jolt at the sight of you like many other animals in the jungle. You're big, but he's bigger. You're strong, but he's stronger. You're armed with razor sharp claws, and four-inch canines, but he's armed with massive horns that'll leave a golf ball sized hole in your abdomen if you're not careful. He's big, he's strong, he's armed, and he's unmoved by your presence. Your only option is to walk out and face him face to face.

Your prey requires sheer power and grit to take down, and that's on a good day. Indeed, he requires nerves of steel in his would-be predators. As you think on these things, you realize that you're the only one reasonably capable of battling such a monster. You've taken down several before, but you were in your prime then. Today, you're much older and much less invigorated. What will you do? Do you risk it all by going in at less than ten percent strength, or do you continue your trek hoping for something a bit smaller along the way? You need to decide! Your pride is fading. They're supercharged for the moment, but soon the adrenaline will die, and they won't be long to follow. You must decide whether to risk or die.

Buffalos are by far the biggest and most formidable prey lions go up against, but because they're so big, the reward of taking one down is bountiful! We all have buffalo-sized desires that we dream of seeing manifested in our lives and in the lives of others. Every man has something deep within him that he thinks about on his drive to work. Every man has something or someone that's on his heart in moments of solitude. These desires, when emanated from a regenerated heart, are rewards. God has already permitted you to secure them because it's His will that they come to light, but we must do something in order to capture them. We must risk trusting Him and relying upon His strength and not our own.

In this chapter, we'll discuss risk-taking and why God wants and even requires us to take big risks. Simply put, dark maned males don't shy away from buffalo-sized rewards. They see reward beyond the risk, and the potential of prolonged provision overshadows the potential of danger.

Hunger Vision

The four leprous men we read about in 2 Kings 7 were in a very similar predicament. They lived in the city of Samaria, which at the time was actively under siege by the Syrian army. It was common war strategy for an army to lay siege around a city, waiting for the citizens of that city to either die of starvation or surrender due to a lack of life-sustaining resources. Samaria was becoming increasingly desperate as the situation grew worse with time. In fact, things got so bad that the people resorted to cannibalism (2 Kings 6:29).

Imagine that! We read of accounts throughout history like this and think to ourselves, "How could they stoop so low? Why didn't they just fight their enemies?" In the comfort of our lives, we sometimes examine history from an unrelatable perspective. We cast judgment upon others because of the decisions they've made without first understanding the reason behind those decisions. It's difficult to grasp the true weight of another's burden while sitting in a coffee shop, enjoying a caramel macchiato with two extra shots of expresso and listening to soft jazz playing in the background. We're too comfortable.

Well, these four leprous men weren't comfortable. They had been ostracized from the general population due to their ailment, hence the reason for them sitting in the gate of the city (2 Kings 7:3). In normal conditions, they would have been forced to leave the city entirely, but considering the circumstances, they were allowed to dwell within the gate. The Bible doesn't tell us how long they had been there, but we can speculate that it had been long enough for them to come to a desperate decision. They were there alone, hungry without any food and comfort long enough for it to become uncomfortable.

Their discomfort was exactly what God used to get them to move in the direction He wanted them to go in. Their hunger and discomfort helped them to see things clearly and to begin entertaining the idea of risk and envisioning the potential of reward. Their lives were brought into perspective as the pain in their abdomen grew sharper, as their bodies grew weaker, and as their hope grew dimmer. I can hear them, saying, "We need to act now! We can't wait any longer!" I can hear them desperately reasoning among each other. I can feel the heat behind their desperate plea for action. I can smell the smoke within their almost consumed expressions. This was a pure life or death situation, and death seemed to be an inevitable outcome no matter which way they turned.

If we say, we will enter into the city, then the famine is in the city, and we shall die there: and if we sit still here, we die also. Now therefore come, and let us fall unto the host of the Syrians: if they save us alive, we shall live; and if they kill us, we shall but die.

2 KINGS 7:4

The desperation they felt eventually pushed them to their breaking point where they made a decision that would change their lives forever. Their decision to leave the city and throw themselves at the mercy of their enemies was the most logical decision they could've made when you consider their options. But as logical as it may have been, it was still a shot in the dark. It was the choice you make when you clearly don't have any better options. It was their absolute last resort, the backup to the backup plan. It was a choice my man Spock from Star Trek would have chosen 10 out of 10 times because it made the most sense. The other two alternatives were sure death sentences, but with this one, there was hope, even if but a little, and it was enough for them to act.

The outcome wasn't a sure one. They weren't one hundred percent on anything. In fact, the odds were stacked against them. They were flying on fumes. They were coasting with no sail. They were driving with no brakes. But even with little likelihood of success, they decided to get up and go anyways, and this is what moves me. The outcome was so impossible to predict yet they went anyways. There's something to be said of men who look not for fair weather as a means for action. There's something to be said of men who'd rather die in action than live in idle discomfort.

The situation had become so dire that anything would be better than staying where they were. They were locked in with their eyes fixed on a possibility. Hunger vision had completely set in, and nothing mattered at this point but action. No excuse would be valid from this point forward. They wouldn't be able to, with good conscience, talk themselves out of this one. It was now or never, go in faith or sit in ruin, risk or die.

We can find ourselves in a similar predicament. No, we may not be suffering from leprosy with a foreign army surrounding our homes and threatening our lives. But life has a way of gradually pushing us into making desperate decisions.

You may be in a dire situation now. Maybe your marriage is suffering, and you can't see the light at the end of the tunnel. Maybe there's a sin that you can't seem to shake, and in the back of your mind, you know that if you don't take action and overcome it, it will eventually ruin you and your family. Or maybe you have a God-ordained dream that hasn't come to past yet, and you know within yourself that if you continue to sit idle on it, it will eventually die. Or perhaps you're someone who's been running away from God your whole life and now your evasion has reached the end of the road. Perhaps the Spirit of God is impressing upon your heart your need to come to Christ, and you know that to ignore Him would be the same as those leprous men deciding to sit idle; it would mean death in the end.

Whatever the predicament you may be in, God requires risk as the only means of getting from A to B. We won't reconcile our relationships with our wives by happenstance. It will require us to risk stepping out of familiar zones and into areas not yet cultivated. We'll have to risk being vulnerable however uncomfortable we may feel. Jesus has already done everything needed to secure your deliverance from the bonds of sin, but you will have to risk letting go of your vices and blindly trust Him to take you on to greater heights in Him. That dream won't come to light on its own. It'll require you to risk your time, talent, and treasure to bring it about for the glory of Almighty God. Coming to Christ will certainly require risk on your part. In fact, I can tell you now that you will suffer loss when you choose to forsake all others and come to Him. There's no way around it. To know Him we must denounce all else.

For whosoever shall save his life shall lose it: and whosoever will lose his life for my sake shall find it.

MATTHEW 16:25

We will risk a literal marring of our reputation, a divide betwixt us and our relationships with people of the world to include friends and family, and a metamorphosis of our most rooted desires. But such losses when compared to the gains inherent in His person ought not to be grieved. John Piper, author of *Risk is Right,* puts it this way, "He is something—someone—worth losing everything for. When we really believe this, then risking everything we are and everything we have, to know and obey Christ is no longer a matter of sacrifice. It's just common sense."[9] The Apostle Paul had this to say:

I count all things but loss for the excellency of the knowledge of Christ Jesus my Lord: for whom I have suffered the loss of all things, and do count them but dung, that I may win Christ.

PHILIPPIANS 3:8

When you're tempted to just sit idle and do nothing in either circumstance, remember those that are counting on you. For just a moment, envision yourself as that lion leading your pride out of famine. How long has it been since you and your family have eaten of the bread of life? Is God's Word apart of your daily diet or is it something foreign? For some lineages, multiple generations may have come and gone since a love for God's Word has been cultivated in their hearts. This is spiritual famine, and it's the worst of its kind.

Take a look to the rear and gaze upon the faces of those that are looking to you to lead them. Are they famished because their spirits have been deprived of God? Remember that they're relying upon you for their daily physical and spiritual provision. They're trusting that you know the way and that you will provide because you're the only one who bears a mane. You're the only one capable of tackling buffalo-sized rewards, such as spiritual maturity manifested within each member of your pride. This should be motivation enough for you to lock in and take on hunger vision.

Hunger vision isn't something you just wake up and have. It's not something you just trip over a rock and fall into. It takes hardship to obtain it, and sometimes that hardship is self-imposed. Sometimes we willfully bear the burdens of sin and disobedience long enough for it to bring us to our knees, and it's not until we're humbled by the weight of our own sin that we begin to consider our predicament.

Like the four leprous – or more fittingly, let's call them courageous men – our discomfort forces us into an ultimatum: either risk or die. We must see the reward ahead of us and possess the courage to go after it, but sometimes the reward doesn't come into vision until we've suffered a little. Though the way may be totally unfamiliar, the idea of gaining a sweeter relationship with our wives, or walking in full deliverance, or living out our calling is what drives us. These are all buffalo-sized rewards that won't come easy. They will require more energy than we may have left. They will demand sheer power and grit to take down, but be of good cheer, because God gives us the power and the grit necessary to capture such rewards. We simply must possess hunger vision, and He promises to take it from there. Once you've fixed your mind upon the buffalo in the distance, and you've begun to close the distance, listen for the chariots of fire, and give heed to the galloping sound of heaven's cavalry!

And they rose up in the twilight, to go unto the camp of the Syrians: and when they were come to the uttermost part of the camp of Syria, behold, there was no man there. For the Lord had made the host of the Syrians to hear a noise of chariots, and a noise of horses, even the noise of a great host.

2 KINGS 7:6

Do you think that heaven began to march before or after the men rose up and began to move? I believe that God ordered His host to move once the four courageous men decided to go. I believe that once they committed to action in their minds, God began to honor their commitment. I believe that as they moved God moved with them, and as we just read, He not only moved with them but He made it so that their footsteps sounded like a mighty army! If you gain nothing else from this chapter, remember that God is in risk.

The Bible presents us with various men who possessed hunger vision. Moses took on hunger vision at the burning bush and would stop at nothing until God was honored in the face of Pharaoh. David became hungry for the glory of God upon hearing the blasphemous words of Goliath of Gath. The Apostle Paul on the road to Damascus. The Apostle Peter at the receipt of Mary Magdalene's message when the Lord was risen. The prodigal son in the pig's pen, and our Lord Jesus as he passed though Samaria to go to Jerusalem. He hungrily sought His crucifixion because He understood what His death would mean for us.

Hunger vision is about locking into the calling God has for your life and pursuing after it hungrily without any reservations, and without any distractions. It's about setting a resolve in your heart to do what God has said no matter what, because you realize that His calling is the only way ahead.

It was the only way the Israelites would know freedom. It's the only way to overcome lion and bear like challenges. It was the only way to reach the gentiles. It was the only way to overcome the guilt of denying the Savior. It's the only way out of the pig's pen and back to the father's house. It was the only way to secure the redemption of all mankind.

Think of it this way: when you're hungry enough, vision will set it in. Men who risk, do so because they need more, hence the acronym Men of Risk (MOR). Straddling the fence unwilling to decide between lukewarm Christianity or a fire hot passion for Christ isn't an option for men who hunger and thirst after righteousness. It's not enough for men who desire to go further, deeper, and higher in Christ. It's not enough for men who covet the dark mane!

Into Darkness

In August of 1866, a Protestant Missionary by the name of Robert Jermain Thomas boarded the *General Sherman*, a US trade ship setting sail to Korea.[10] Previous to this, he had endured the death of his wife and fellow missionary partner, Caroline Godfrey, due to a sudden miscarriage while living abroad and serving as missionaries in Shanghai, China. Discouraged, Robert forsook the mission field and settled for work as a customs officer in Chefoo, China. During his time there, he met two Korean fisherman who were eager to own a Bible.

Korea was not divided at this time, and the nation was completely opposed to foreign ideology to include the Christian faith. To own a Bible would have been considered a treasure to some because of its rarity in the country, but if caught with one, execution was a common punishment. Upon learning of the Korean people's need for more Bibles, Robert determined that he would go. Hunger vision began to set in! There was a need for more, and though that need was not a personal one for Robert, it was a need nonetheless.

Robert knew full well the risks associated with his travels to Korea but decided to go anyway. His first visit lasted four months, during which he managed to smuggle in many Bibles without detection. After the four months, he departed from Korea due to it becoming too dangerous for foreigners. Still, he felt that his mission and calling to the Korean people was not fulfilled. There was still a hunger to reach the people of the hermit kingdom, and so he sought another opportunity to return.

His second trip proved fatal. In 1866, Robert learned that an American ship, the *General Sherman*, was going to try to establish trade relations between Korea and the United States. He was permitted to board the ship as an interpreter in exchange for a chance to smuggle more Bibles into Korea.

While aboard the *General Sherman,* the foreign trade ship was unwelcomed and consequently attacked by the Korean people as it sailed up the Taedong River toward Pyongyang. The ship was set ablaze, forcing Robert and the crew aboard to jump ship only to be met with men armed with machetes. Robert was killed at the hand of a Korean man, but before his death, history records something truly remarkable. As his executioner stood before him, Robert did something not many would have possessed the gall to do. In his last moment, he offered the man a Bible as he exclaimed, "Jesus, Jesus," in the Korean language.

Imagine that! This is how far hunger vision can take a man. It will literally drive us into utter darkness all for the glory of God. Robert was so fixed on his calling to reach the hermit kingdom that it didn't matter what obstacles were set before him. He was willing to risk it all to ensure that he fulfilled his God-given calling to reach the Korean people with the gospel. He literally went into darkness with this one thing in mind, and though he died, he is remembered as the first Protestant missionary to reach Korea with the lifechanging gospel of Jesus Christ. Following Robert's death, a mandate was published by the Korean government to have all copies of the Bible destroyed. Many obeyed with the exception of at least one government official named Pak Yong-Sik. Pak took his copy of the Bible and decided to use many of its pages as wallpaper in his home.

People from far and wide came to his home to read the strange book plastered on the walls. Fifteen years after Robert's death, there sprouted over 100 churches in the capitol of Korea. Today, South Korea is comprised of over 40 percent Christians! Robert's death certainly wasn't in vain, and neither was his risk.

Four

———

The Hopcraft Effect

And he shall be like a tree planted by the rivers of water, that bringeth forth his fruit in his season.

PSALM 1:3

THERE'S A WORD THAT GETS THROWN AROUND THE Church more than baseballs at a Yankees' game. We make sure to include it in our prayers for others and ourselves. We use this word when greeting one another and when parting ways. We even speak this word over our meals. It's a word that encompasses divine favor, mercy, grace, protection, provision, and anything else good you can think of. Are you ready for this? The word is blessing, to include each of its variations.

There's not a person on earth today that doesn't want to live a blessed life. We all want the favor of God upon our lives, whether we admit it or not. We all wish to have our families protected and provided for every single day. We desire to live long healthy lives full of great experiences, joy, and peace. Yet many of us are not pleased with our lives. For many, life is not as blessed as we would like it to be. We're unhappy and unsatisfied and can never seem to understand why.

Well, according to Psalm 1, a blessed life has its conditions, meaning it doesn't happen automatically. We all have the potential to live a life of blessing, but we must take ownership of our own decisions and acknowledge that we're more than likely contributing to our own dissatisfaction. We like to look externally and point fingers at outward circumstances and people as the reason behind our unhappiness. But we know that, when the onion is peeled all the way back, it's we who are to blame. It's always personal. It's always the man in the mirror. Take a look at this psalm and pay close attention to the man's positioning:

Blessed is the man that walketh not in the counsel of the ungodly, nor standeth in the way of sinners, nor sitteth in the seat of the scornful.

PSALM 1:1

Positioning

Positioning is paramount to every man's spiritual maturity and development. Where and with whom we position ourselves will directly impact our fruitfulness. Our associations with people and the places we choose to inhabit have a real potential of positively or negatively affecting the shade of our manes. We're either helped or hindered by our fellowship.

The man spoken of in Psalm 1 is a blessed man simply because he's mindful and wary of his positioning. He's selective of the counsel he receives from others because he understands that counsel is the root of direction. Where we find ourselves five, ten, or twenty years from now will always trace back to the counsel, whether sound or ill, we received and adhered to early on (Proverbs 20:18).

Remember what God asked Adam in the garden? Adam and Eve hid themselves from the presence of God because of their sin, and while in hiding, the Lord sought for them. Adam responds to the voice of God and says in Genesis 3:10, "I heard thy voice in the garden, and I was afraid, because I was naked." God never told Adam that he was naked so immediately God noticed a red flag. He must've received that information from someone or something else. God responds in verse 11, "Who told thee that thou wast naked? Hast thou eaten of the tree, whereof I commanded thee that thou shouldest not eat?" God was digging for the root! In fear, Adam blames the woman for his actions, and Eve also fearing, contributes her unwise decision to the serpent when questioned by God.

And the woman said, the serpent beguiled me, and I did eat.

GENESIS 3:13

Herein lies the root of the issue at hand. That sinful bite of the fruit traces back to the moment Eve stopped and listened to the voice of the serpent. His counsel was all that was needed to get her moving in the direction he wanted. God's concern was with the origin of the bad counsel Adam had adhered to. He wanted to know exactly where Adam got his information and who had Adam's ear.

God cares about who we're listening to. He's concerned with who we allow to advise us because counsel is the root of direction. Yet so often people turn to inadequate sources for advice. People foolishly turn to all sorts of mediums for counsel when they're going through a rough patch in life, when they could just as easily turn to God. Instead of seeking and finding the wisdom of God, they turn to books written by popular authors, they listen to people who have amassed the riches of this world, they adhere to the words of the ungodly, and they do this all in the hopes of living a blessed life. But the evidence of a blessed life is not marked by how many followers you have on social media, or how many books you've sold, or how many assets you have to your name. A blessed life is determined by how obedient we are to God's Word, and if it's His Word that we're evading, then we ought not to expect the blessings of God to come by any other means.

Adam and Eve removed themselves from their rightful position of obedience when they adhered to the counsel of the serpent, and consequently it altered both their direction and ours. Now, we can see in hindsight and trace the world's sin problem back to the counsel they adhered to in the beginning. Simply put, counsel influences our positioning which in turn determines whether or not our lives are blessed and fruitful or cursed and barren.

Planted in Truth

The man mentioned in Psalm 1 doesn't associate himself with ungodly men. He doesn't walk in their counsel, he doesn't stand united with them in sin, and he doesn't sit contentedly in the dimness of their company. He has absolutely no interest in the vices and cruel company of the world and verse two reveals why:

*But his delight is in the law of the Lord; and in his law doth he
meditate day and night.*

PSALM 1:2

He takes extreme satisfaction in the Word of God. Because
of God's Word, he and the ungodly share no common interests. The law of God living and breathing in his heart is the
only thing that distinguishes him from his sinful neighbors.
Without it, he would be no different and would naturally find
comfort and familiarity in their company. But because of his
love for God's Word, he is severed from the fellowship of
darkness and therefore removed from their company. He is
totally consumed by a desire for God's Word to the point that
it's all that he thinks about. His mind is completely given over
to the scriptures, and this is the underlining reason for his
blessed life. He isn't blessed because of anything about himself – his achievements, characteristics, or his luck as many
would claim – but rather because the Word of God itself is
blessed and he's chosen to cleave to it.

The Word of God is blessed by itself. It's blessed because it
originated with and proceeded from God. When we hear and
obey these blessed words, we too become blessed because of
the words.

Blessed are they that hear the word of God, and keep it.

LUKE 11:28

The blessings of God are conditional. That may be a hard
pill to swallow for some, but it's true. His blessings hinge

upon our obedience to His Word. Becoming a man capable of bearing a dark mane will require obedience on your part. That mane won't darken on its own. The fruit of God's Spirit within you won't develop on its own either. You will have to delight in God's Word and partake of only what is pure. You will have to plant yourself in Him. This means you will have to allow His Word to become the foundation of your life: what you eat, think, and live day in and day out. You may think, "I hear you, but my life is too busy to be that committed. I have a family, a career, and so many more responsibilities that require my time and energy."

Our lives are never so busy that we can't set aside time to spend with God. It's always a matter of what we deem as important and not. It's a matter of priority. Yes, spending time with our families and attending to our responsibilities as husbands, fathers, and men are important, but they're not nearly as vital as ensuring we feed our inner man the only thing capable of satisfying his hunger; if he goes hungry, so does everyone, and everything else!

As a husband and father of three, I've come to grips with the fact that I can't lead my family and be the spiritual leader they need me to be when I've chosen to undermine my time with God. Family time is important, but nothing ranks above God-time. I'm an advocate for spending quality family time, and I know it's essential to influencing the family unit in the ways of righteousness, but I also understand that when the family is prioritized above God, it's only a matter of time before it begins to crumble and break apart.

It's when we've planted ourselves in the truth found in God's Word that our perspective becomes clear and we gain the wisdom needed to prioritize everyone and everything in our lives properly – as God would have us. When we've purposed to position ourselves strategically, avoiding ungodly associations that yield no fruit and putting down roots in habitats of holiness, we'll gradually begin to see the shade of our manes changing, darkening, and deepening in color. Our level of spiritual maturity will begin to increase dramatically, thus enabling us to lead others along, *The Way of the Mane.*

Choosing Habitat Wisely

Dr. Grant Hopcraft, one of the world's leading wildlife researchers sought to discover the method behind how lions choose their habitat based on hunting opportunities. He and his team used long-term radio-telemetry data collected over the course of 16 years in their effort to determine whether lions choose habitat based on prey availability or prey accessibility. I think our natural tendency is to assume that lions choose their habitat based on areas that have the greatest prey density; wherever prey is most prevalent would be the best place for a lion to live. Right?

Well, instead of making assumptions, Dr. Hopcraft relied solely upon the data he and his team collected. As a method of gathering information, Dr. Hopcraft went to every site a radio collared lion was known to have killed a prey animal and he measured the height of the grass within that area. This was done because grass height in the plains is indicative of high or low prey density. Ungulates graze the open plains, so if the grass is low, it suggests that there's a higher presence of prey, and if the grass is high, it suggests just the opposite. If the data revealed that lions spent majority of their time in locations where the grass was short, it would mean that they prefer to dwell in areas of high prey density – areas where prey animals are commonly found.

After following this formula for almost two decades, the numbers revealed something unexpected. It turned out that lions actually prefer to live in places where prey animals are rarely sighted. Strange, isn't it? Go to the area where prey is hardly ever seen and wait it out? Seems like it's the worst of the two methods, but there's a reasonable explanation.

Lions are sit-and-wait predators, which means they must exercise great patience in the hunting process. They're not as quick and agile as leopards or cheetahs who find great success in hunting down prey in the open plains. Lions are big and heavy, so for the majority of the time, they depend upon the ambush to catch prey that is quicker of foot. The use of concealment and acceleration are two techniques they rely upon greatly.

Dr. Hopcraft discovered that the land area where two rivers meet, also known as a confluence, is prime territory for lions. Such areas provide an adequate amount of vegetation suitable for concealment, and as he states in his article, *Planning for Success: Serengeti Lions Seek Prey Accessibility Rather than Abundance,* "Access to water provides predictable locations for encountering prey."[11] The key word in that statement is predictable. Though prey animals are scarcely sighted in said locations due to the high risk associated with grazing in an enclosed space, lions can predict their coming based on natural history. They know through experience that the prey will come to the water eventually, and it's upon this understanding that they wait. Though the prey is not immediately available in these confluences, lions instinctively trust that their provision will come, and so they wait for God to provide by natural course.

For we walk by faith, not by sight.

2 CORINTHIANS 5:7

Lions exercise great faith in the hunting process. Field studies have revealed that prides that choose to dwell by these major confluences have a greater likelihood of success than those that seek their prey in the plains. It takes great faith to sit and wait on something that is not in plain sight, especially when your belly is rumbling. They know where their provision comes from. They know that so long as they position themselves strategically their meat will come by the hand of God. This is the sort of faith they possess, and we can learn from them.

The young lions roar after their prey, and seek their meat from God.

PSALM 104:21

This Christian life that we've decided to embark upon requires faith from start to finish. We too must sit and wait on the promises and provision of God. We too must choose our habitat wisely and determine whether it's wiser to chase what is immediately available or wait on something far better. This reminds me of the great patriarchs of the Christian faith recorded in the eleventh chapter of the book of Hebrews. Hebrews 11:13 tells us, "These all died in faith, not having received the promises, but having seen them afar off, and were persuaded of them, and confessed that they were strangers and pilgrims on the earth." As Christians, we are walking in the steps of men and women who lived wisely and chose to cleave unto God and His promises rather than become consumed with inordinate affections for the things of this world. We ought to walk this way as we follow Jesus, trusting in His Word and His providence.

Like all creation, lions know their Creator and His design for their lives. Dark-maned males choose to forsake the plains and dwell by the river because they trust that their Creator will feed them. Just as sure as the rising of the sun, those prey animals are eventually drawn by nature to the river. God literally sends them by natural course into the paw of the lion, and all the lion must do is wait patiently for his provision.

I was in the passenger seat of a good brother's pickup truck in route to a fishing hole down in Augusta, Georgia. As he drove through the countryside, I noticed out my window a beautiful sight. As I looked, I saw a clearly well fed and well-groomed dog sprawled out in front of his master's estate, and he appeared not to have a single care in the world. What made this sighting so profound to me wasn't that he simply lay there but that he wasn't chained to a fence or post and neither was there any leash about his neck, yet he stayed. It was in his power to up and run off into the country had he desired to, but it was clear he wanted to be there. It was about eight fifteen on a Saturday morning when I saw him. He lay contentedly, centered on his master's wraparound driveway just at the brink where the asphalt met the lawn. I mentioned the sighting to the brother as he drove, and we began to speak joyfully of the spiritual application.

You see, like that dog, we too have the capacity to reach a place in our lives where we belong. Like that dog, we too can discover the blessedness of having a Master that provides all of our needs no matter how small or great. My brother and I began to imagine what life must've been like for that dog for him to visibly display such satisfaction. He probably didn't know exactly what time his master would feed him, but he knew that he would be fed that day. Otherwise, he would've run off in search for scraps like many of his fellows. He was in no wise a stray dog but rather a dog that had found a home and could rest and rely upon the faithfulness of his master. As we talked more, we began to wonder of the many stray dogs out there having to search for their food every hour of every day. Sometimes, they find something, but often, they go hungry, and this contributes to their overall appearance and attitude.

You can spot a stray whenever you see one. He's filthy from tail to snout. The outline of his ribcage can be seen behind his scruffy fur. He trots with his head constantly on a swivel, looking for anything that'll temporarily silence the hunger pain in his belly. He lives a rough life all his days, but this isn't the case with the dog who finds his home. What a difference positioning makes in the life of any creature!

I'm not calling you a dog, brother. I'm simply saying that we must quit running in our own strength and knowledge and begin to do what's wise and find our place in Christ. You and I see men every day that look like a stray. You can spot him when you see him. His thoughts are filthy and so is his speech as a result. He doesn't honor God in any aspect of his life. He hangs with ungodly and undone men like himself. He walks about with his head on the swivel constantly looking for another woman, another fix, another thing to temporarily silence the hunger that's deep down in his soul. He brags about the number of women he's had sex with as if it's a badge of honor, when he should be ashamed. He should be sprawled out on the floor weeping over the many women he's manipulated emotionally, but instead, he boasts. He continues to chase his next fix, and as time goes on, that hunger in his soul only deepens. The favor of God is not with him and so he lives a rough life all his days, but this isn't the case with those of us who have found our home in Christ. Those of us that, like the patriarchs of our faith, chose to put down roots in Christ and wait on His unfailing promises.

Are you willing to wait patiently for the provision and promises of God? Is God not more faithful than nature itself? God is faithful to provide whatever you have need of. Do you have a dream that hasn't come to light? It's likely God is trying to get your attention so that He can direct you to the confluence away from the plains first. God wills that you first undergo a transformation of the heart, because it's then that your desires will begin to change. That dream that you have now may not be what God has planned for your life. It's best to get rooted in Him first and allow Him to change your heart before you begin to dream. Once you've developed a love for Him and His Word, His house, and His people, then dream big because then your dreams will align with His will for your life. How long are you willing to wait? Is there a desire within you for a pride of your own? How long are you willing to sit still? Maybe God has already entrusted to you a family of your own, and you're trying to figure out how to properly lead them. Are you ready to sit quietly and hear the master? Are you lacking in spiritual strength? Again, how long are you able to just sit and wait.

Dark maned males learn to sit and wait for their provision to come to them as opposed to wasting valuable energy chasing after something that's virtually impossible to catch. Their positioning couldn't be more spot on. The river provides everything they need.

Come to the River

Putting down roots in a place where the resources you require are hardly seen seems to go against reason. But like the Serengeti lions, we must possess more vision than logic. We must have more foresight than short sight. We can reason our way out of anything, but dark maned males possess the unique capability of seeing provision before it arrives. Foresight is twenty-twenty when your positioning is proper.

When we've made the river our dwelling place, like the man mentioned in Psalm 1, we will eventually produce fruit. The Psalmist says in verse three of that first chapter, "And he shall bring forth his fruit in his season." He trusts the process. Dark maned males live a life of faith not reason. We trust that our supply will come so long as we remain riverside, because God is faithful and He has promised to provide. This is the life of faith Jesus is calling us to live. It's a life of total dependency upon Him. His will is that we come to the river where all our needs will be met.

How often did Jesus beckon for men to follow Him, and how often did they refuse? Many of them allowed reasoning to keep them from following Him. They were misled by rational thinking that says, "My immediate needs prevent me from going after Him. I'd be better off pursuing some other certain gain than in hoping for something I cannot see." Like lions who choose to dwell in habitats where prey is most abundant, these men were misled by their own eyes and couldn't see that an immediate abundance doesn't always equate to a perpetual supply.

Many times, men chase after what catches the eye. Immediate provision, such as fast women, fast money, and fast power, allures our attention. We want what pleases our senses right now. We don't want to wait until we're married before we share in intercourse. We don't want to trust God with our finances and work to sustain a living and support our families. We don't want to go through the training and hard experience required for us to become leaders of character and integrity. We want to achieve the next promotion as quickly as possible, and we don't pause to consider the benefits of being processed. In our sensually dulled minds, we value what is instant over what is constant. But the instant gratifications of our flesh are a well that always runs dry, thus keeping us on the chase. God promises us a constant supply. But we want it all right now, and the world does a great job of setting it all before our eyes.

We have to realize that while chasing instant satisfaction is immediately satisfying, it keeps you on the chase, nonetheless. When do you rest? When does your soul rest? Wouldn't you rather sit and wait peacefully for your provision? Wouldn't you rather expend less energy on more substance than more energy on no substance?

Christ isn't directing us to follow Him as we tend to our own things. If that were His intent, then why would there be any need for us to follow Him? Following Him means that we trust Him to attend to our needs as we follow Him. It means that we're okay with sitting and waiting on Him to do what He has promised. Following Him requires us to exercise faith in Him, and this is where most men hesitate.

Most men find it hard to relinquish control over to another because our lives, from our perspectives, are our own. We prefer to think on our own, to lead on our own, and ultimately to live on our own accord. But there comes a time when we have to acknowledge the fact that we need help. There comes a time when we have to accept that we don't do so well on our own. If, by the grace of God, we're able to come to this state of humility, we will have to make a decision that will alter the course of our lives forever. We will have to choose either to follow Jesus or continue to attend to our own things.

And he said unto another, Follow me. But he said, Lord, suffer me first to go and bury my father. Jesus said unto him, let the dead bury their dead: but go thou and preach the kingdom of God. And another also said, Lord, I will follow thee; but let me first go and bid them farewell, which are at home at my house.

LUKE 9:59-61

These men, in the verses above, lacked the faith needed to propel them into a life of blessing. They were still thinking that following Jesus could wait. How terrible of an idea! Such men are comparable to lions who lack the vision needed to see value in a seemingly scarce environment. These men undermined the power of God when they refused to follow Him. Much like habitats that at first glance lack prey, Jesus was and still is often seen by many as someone who could never provide what we have need of. They say He's too archaic, His principles too dated. They say His Words have no place in modern society. People see Him as a strange wilderness they'd rather not inhabit. Men view Him this way because they possess carnal minds. Their positioning is off and, as a result, so is their vision. They fail to see the immense value that He adds to our lives because this value can only be spiritually discerned (1 Corinthians 2:14).

Make no mistake about it; there is nothing scarce or outdated about Christ. He is the fulfillment of all that we could ever need or desire. We're the ones that view Him as less than who He is. We're the ones with obscured vison, often blinded by the deceitfulness of abundant pleasures found in the world. It's not until we choose to make Him our habitation that we perceive just how sure of a foundation and shelter He is.

I'm always looking for an opportunity to invite someone to church service or fellowship. The house of God is where all men need to be on a consistent basis. I think this way firstly because the Word of God mandates it and secondly because mine and my family's life was completely changed when we began to frequent the house of God.

Prior to prioritizing God's house and purposing to serve in His ministry, I was a wreck – to put it simply. I didn't have a consistent prayer life, my love for my wife and daughter was not there, and I was spiritually starving. My positioning was off. The man on the inside – the lion within – was hungry. I was starving because I was searching for resources in the open plain when I should have been sitting contentedly waiting by the river.

We try to find all the answers to our internal hunger in self-help books, podcasts, friends, social validation on social media, and the list can go on. But the answers can only be found in Jesus; they can only be found by the river. I wasn't living a life of faith. My day-to-day life was being dictated by the interests and cravings of my flesh, and this was contributing greatly to my lack of fruit.

Long story short, by the grace of God, we quickly migrated to the river. I had become fed up with not being fed and would no longer consent to my own spiritual starvation. I needed to be in God's house! I needed to read my Bible! I needed to pray! I needed to prioritize the will of God for my life above my own will! My hunger for holiness and true righteousness began to propel me forward in Christ.

Sound familiar?

Hunger vision was completely set in! This was the season my inner man caught fire, and he's been burning ever since. The burden of my own sin-laden life crushed me into an ultimatum: either risk or starve! I had to either risk walking with Jesus on the waters or continue to stand by idle in the boat of my own despair and shame. I had to risk migrating away from the plains I had grown so accustomed to inhabiting. These plains seemingly provided an abundant supply of the resources I would need to be a better, more refined individual. Resources such as success in business, fame, physical fitness, personal achievement, a higher education, and you fill in the rest. Why dwell by the river and wait on something that may never come when I can pursue prey now? Make no mistake, all these pursuits just mentioned are fine and dandy when they're second to the will of God. In fact, these pursuits are likely achieved when the will of God is priority in our lives; they're often what God adds to us when we've sought after His Kingdom and righteousness first (Matthew 6:33).

The world seemingly provides an abundance of resources for us to capture in the pursuit of becoming a better man. But when a man seeks to improve himself by worldly means and does not consider his spiritual needs, he is actually going nowhere and doing nothing. We can achieve every goal we set out to accomplish, we can reach the highest of worldly education, and we can build the biggest company and earn so much money that we don't know what to do with it all. But God is very clear about His views on worldly gain:

For what is a man profited, if he shall gain the whole world,
and lose his own soul? or what shall a man give in exchange
for his soul?

MATTHEW 16:26

In terms of progression and personal development and achievement, God places precedence upon the soul: the man on the inside. At the end of the day, after exhausting all of my energy, I always ended up hungry. No pursuit I had undertaken, no progress I had made, and no achievement I had acquired ever fed the hunger that came from down deep. I was doing a lot of running but not covering any ground. I was actively on the hunt every day, but I never captured any real substance.

If we're intent on living a blessed life – which if you're reading this book, I believe you are – then it's clear we will have to migrate to the river. We will need to dwell within the confluence of God's house which provides all the resources we need in order to develop our manes.

The Confluence of God's House

You may have heard at one point or another God's house referred to as a hospital for the sick. This is an accurate analogy of what God's house represents for those who are spiritually ailing. But what happens when the spiritually sick have recovered and are now made whole? What then does the Church represent for them? Are they to leave and return to the place that made them vile in the first place? What then does the Church become? It becomes a confluence. Have you ever heard the Church referred to as a confluence? Probably not. Well, when we consider what a confluence actually is, the church fits the mold to a tee.

Merriam defines it as *a coming or flowing together, meeting, or gathering at one point.*[12]

That's the Church!

Earlier, I stated that a confluence is the land area where two rivers meet. It's a place that provides dense vegetation due to its abundant water supply. Lions thrive in these areas, especially in the dry season when prey are forced to migrate to the river.

Dr. Hopcraft found these areas to be where several prides spent most of their time over the 16-year study period. The prides that chose these confluences as their home were better off due to the access to prey as well as the abundant water supply in the dry season. Female lion reproductive rates were overwhelmingly higher in these areas as opposed to the plains. Everything from more opportunity for food, more shelter for the cubs, and more water were key perks in dwelling riverside.

The lions that preferred the open plains struggled due to there being an inadequacy of concealment and lack of prey and water in the dry season. Their positioning was off! Areas outside of these confluences can be harsh on any pride. Though in the wet season, there's an abundance of prey that stand right before their eyes, the lions are unable to capture them because the open environment doesn't support their created design. In like manner, the world and places of the world don't support our Christian design. Jesus very clearly states in John 15:19, "I have called you out of the world."

There comes a time when we as Christian men have to come to terms with who we are. We will have to accept either our former identity or our new identity in Christ and resolutely walk in it. We will have to determine within our own individual minds what sort of lion we are; do we prefer the plains – which ironically enough is that of a plain, unfruitful life – or the river? If Jesus has called us out of something, it's because He intends to place us into something else. He doesn't call us out of the world so that we can just live on our own in isolation, being an island to ourselves. We still require an abode. We still require a place of shelter where we can effectively secure what we need. God's house is the confluence needed to capture the resources required for us to bear fruit – for us to develop dark manes.

Those that be planted in the house of the Lord shall flourish in the courts of our God. They shall still bring forth fruit in old age, they shall be fat and flourishing.

PSALM 92:13-14

The Church is gold to the man whose mind has been spiritually renewed but plastic to the man of the world. He can't

see the value in going to worship a God he can't physically see. He thinks of it as foolishness and a complete waste of
time. It's time he could spend sleeping, drinking, partying,
reading, spending, or wasting with other people of the world.
But for you and me, the Church is precious because it's the
house of our Father and a catalyst for producing fruit.

Notice how the yielding of fruit is directly linked to being planted in God's house. The psalmist clearly identifies the
cause for the fruit being produced when he says, "Those that
be planted in the house of the Lord.

When a seed is planted, it means that it's firmly set in
place, properly positioned to bear fruit. This is the attitude
we should have toward the house of God. This was David's
attitude and lifelong commitment.

Surely goodness and mercy shall follow me all the days of my life:
and I will dwell in the house of the Lord forever.

PSALM 23:6

I meet men all the time who lightly attend church service.
They may fellowship on special events such as Memorial Day
barbeques or on other major holidays, but their inconsistency reveals their unwillingness to be planted in God's house.
They're not planted, and that's the reason they don't grow.
They haven't established roots in God's house. They aren't set
in place. More fittingly, they're like seeds that are occasional-
ly set upon the soil's surface that blow away with every slight
gust of wind. Because they're not rooted in the Church, they
can't understand the value of the Church. Remember what
I said earlier: *The Church is gold to the man whose mind has*

been spiritually renewed, but plastic to the man of the world.

When we, through faith, make a conscious decision to be planted in the house of the Lord, and we purpose to walk in obedience to His Word, we will eventually produce fruit. It has to happen. The soil is too rich for us not to produce fruit. But it takes faith on our part. Men who see the Church as plastic may come to one or two services a month, and it makes sense why they do. Such a man is not expecting to gain anything from God because he's not planted. But if he, professing to be a Christian, rarely visits his Father's house, it raises some questions: What else has his heart? Where else is he planted? If we're not in the house of God, where are we? What other place is a more appropriate habitation for the Christian man other than his own home? Where should we be spending our time if not in the house of God among the people of God? If we view God's house as a strange place and find that our desire is to be elsewhere, then what does that reveal about us? Shouldn't our Father's house be home in every sense, especially when we have a healthy understanding of what He provides for us in His house?

For a day in thy courts is better than a thousand. I had rather be a doorkeeper in the house of my God, than to dwell in tents of wickedness.

PSALM 84:10

It's my understanding that a man willing to suffer less when more is readily at his hand is a man that has great and notable reason. The psalmist boldly professes that he'd prefer to stand and face the elements with God than sit in a heated tent without Him. I can tell you from personal experience, having trained in the field, that the tent is where everyone wants to be in the winter. Heat is the single most important resource other than food when you're out there. Every soldier's mind is on the heat in the tent all throughout a day of training. So, there must be something incredibly beneficial about God's house that would convince a man to suffer in order to reserve his place with God. Such a man must have great and notable reasons as to why he'd rather suffer with God than flourish with man.

God's house is a confluence for us. It's where we gather the resources necessary to produce healthy, full, awe-inspiring manes for God's glory. It's where growth inevitably takes place if in fact we are planted. The Hopcraft effect speaks to a faith-lead life. It's about being properly positioned for thy mane's sake.

Five

Teach Him to Reason

Then said I, Wisdom is better than strength...

ECCLESIASTES 9:16

EVERY SO OFTEN, I'M PRIVILEGED WITH AN OPPORTUNITY to speak to a group of predominately male soldiers, and I always purpose to mention the lion. At some point during my speaking, I pose a question to the group, "When you hear the word 'lion,' what adjectives come to mind?" Without fail, they shout out words such as fearless, courageous, bold, royal, strong, among other commonly thought descriptions of the lion. My next question is always the same: "Okay, now when you hear the word 'hyena,' what words do you think of?" Again, without fail, they give descriptive words such as cowardice, weak, follower, ugly, scavenger, and so on.

Once we've determined the blatant difference and absolute contrast between the two beasts, they're ready for my final question. As the room is silent and everyone is attentive, anticipating the point behind it all, I simply ask, "Which are you?"

You see, we must decide what sort of man we're going to

be for ourselves. We must determine whether we're going to lead or follow, and we have to take into account the consequences of our decision either way. Every decision we make will have effects that follow. These effects will inevitably touch the next generation of mane-bearers, so it's imperative we think long and hard about who exactly we're going to be. Such thought is necessary if we're to lead lives of fruitfulness and please the Lord in all that we do.

As often as I've asked these questions to groups of men, never once did any man ever think the lion to be wise. No one ever described the lion as a wise creature. Lions and wisdom don't commonly go together. We don't associate the king of beasts with clear thought. They're only thought of as beasts – wild and reckless brutes that totally live by impulse.

But lions have been around since the beginning of creation. They've overcome the odds of survival time and time again. They've been forced out of habitation by human infrastructure. They've been poisoned by herdsmen. They've been speared by adrenaline-stricken tribesmen. They've been hunted, shot down, and stuffed by affluent trophy hunters. For millenniums, they've been trapped, captured, and ripped from their prides all in the name of human entertainment, and still they sit at the top of the food chain. You don't overcome that much adversity by strength alone. Consider what Derick Joubert, a writer for the National Geographic, has to say regarding lion resilience, "Even with their thinning numbers, it's nonetheless something of a miracle that despite human firepower—from spears to carbofuran poison (a crop pesticide) to .375 rifles to wire snares—these murderous animals have managed to endure."[13]

Ponder Thy Paw

Ponder the path of thy feet and let all thy ways be established.

PROVERBS 4:26

Lions have overcome the uneven odds of survival primarily due to their instincts. For the most part, they instinctively make good decisions. Dark maned males are such because they instinctively consider their abode. They've overcome the odds because of where they choose to dwell. Location is essential to the short and long-term success of any pride.

Male lions have every incentive to bear a dark mane. The mane attracts females and increases a male's mating opportunity. Female lions take little interest in males with shaggy, light manes because it's open advertisement of a male who struggles to take care of himself, let alone a pride. It's simple logic to the lioness. If he can't properly feed himself, then there's no way their cubs will have a chance.

The same is true for young men. Women desire men who they believe can properly take care of their needs both current and future. When they see a man, they think to themselves, "Is he husband and father material?" At first glance, they're already thinking long-term because a woman desires commitment. Whether she's a Christian woman or not, she desires a man who possess the fruit of the Spirit. She may not realize that's what she wants, but it is. She wants a man that's booming with fruit, a man that bears a dark mane showing forth spiritual power and strength. I'm getting ahead of myself! We'll talk more about this in chapter eight, "The Mane Attraction."

The point I'm making is the darker the mane the more attractive the male because the mane means something. It validates his ability to lead and reveals his level of masculinity. Though there's much reason to bear a mane and it's what every male lion needs, it's incredibly difficult to develop one separate from a major river confluence. Lions who live separate from major confluences tend to develop what's known as manelessness, and it's exactly how it sounds. A combination of overexposure to hot climates and an inconsistent diet are what contribute to lion baldness.

Anna Mosser was a graduate student on Packer's team when she compiled all the data taken from the radio collars used during the study period. This she did to map out the lion's typical reproductive rates over the 16-year study phase. After collecting the data, she developed a Darwinian real estate map which displayed areas of the Serengeti that were high in reproductive success, and other areas that were not.

And the results were clear: "Decade after decade, reproductive rates were highest for lions that occupied the confluence along the major rivers."[14]

Simply put, lion cubs rarely survive in areas separate from these major confluences. Life is rough out on the plains. Cubs need the safety of the river as their abode if they're to grow well-nourished and fed.

Let that sink in for a bit.

In chapter 4, "The Hopcraft Effect," we learned that confluences are prime real estate for lions. We also learned that the Church can be likened unto these confluences because of how much of a necessity the Church is for every Christian man. It's not just a nutrient needed for us to produce fruit, but it is the ground within which we are planted. We must make it a point to keep our children in the house of God regularly. The Word of God preached, the fellowship of the saints, and the overall Christian community is what we leverage in our bid to help them produce fruit at some point down the line. But how many guys have we met that grew up in the Church all their lives and are still lacking fruit? I'm sure we can name off several; I used to be one of those guys.

This typically happens when the Church and home don't look the same. This happens when the man Junior sees at church isn't the same man he sees at home. Our homes must flow together with the temple. If we're kind to everyone we mingle with in the house of God, we must be kind to our families at home. If we're quick to serve others in the house of God, we must be quick to serve the needs of our families when we're home. If we're patient with our brothers and sisters in Christ, we must be patient with our wives and children. The moment they notice an imbalance – and their sixth sense picks up even the slightest sign of two-sided or coin-like character – you could potentially lose your witness.

When you speak to them and try to teach them biblical principles, they may be reluctant to listen. Coin-like character causes us to lose all credibility. They subconsciously think within their heart, "If he doesn't believe, why should I?" Remember, as the mane-bearer of your home, you are the primary example they're looking to; if you don't practice what you preach, neither will they. Our inconsistent life is enough evidence to prove that we're not one hundred percent on board with God's way. If we're to prepare the next generation of mane-bearers, we will have to not only lay down roots in the Church but we will have to be the Church. We will have to take a long hard look at our pawprints behind us and consider where they lead.

We should ask ourselves:

- Am I leading my pride into a life of fruitfulness?

- Does my home life flow with my Church life?

- Does my pride respect me enough to adhere to what I teach them?

If the respect isn't there, it's likely that you've lost your credibility. If this sounds like you, don't lose heart! You can always begin again. You can regain the confidence of your family by showing yourself consistent in and outside of the home. It'll take prayer and effort on your part, but it's worth it.

Brains Over Brawn

If you're even slightly familiar with King Solomon, you'd know that he's primarily known for the wisdom he received from God. At the dawn of his tenure as king of Israel, Solomon impressed God with his heart. God had given him an opportunity to ask anything of Him, and instead of asking for selfish things like more riches or power, Solomon asked for wisdom and knowledge. More than anything, he wanted to lead the people of God in a way that would please God and effectively fulfill his responsibility as king. His answer revealed his heart, and God was pleased with his response.

In that night did God appear unto Solomon, and said unto him, Ask what I shall give thee. And Solomon said unto God, Thou hast shewed great mercy unto David my father, and hast made me to reign in his stead. Now, O Lord God, let thy promise unto David my father be established: for thou hast made me a king over a people like the dust of the earth in multitude. Give me now wisdom, and knowledge, that I may go out and come in before this people: for who can judge this thy people, that is so great?

2 CHRONICLES 1:7-10

Solomon's heart was in the right place. He was approaching his responsibility to the throne with a sober mind, desiring to lead effectively for the glory of God. He knew that more riches wouldn't aid him in exercising sound judgement. Silver and gold are poor companions when discretion is called upon and required for effective leadership. I've never known a dollar to offer sound counsel in the hour of decision making.

Instead of asking God for the life of his enemies, Solomon desired the wisdom needed to overcome them. He wasn't looking for the easy way out of his responsibility; he was intent on going the hard way in – the hard way into a tenure of effective leadership. He wasn't a check the block sort of man; he wanted to hit the mark. He wanted to make a lasting impact on Israel, and this is why I say he went the hard way in.

If we're to achieve godly results in our lives and the lives of our children, we will have to trek the way less traveled. The path of least resistance will always be the easy way out of a life of true impact. Upholding God's standard of righteousness is not popular, and it never will be. We will be faced with resistance from those that are of the world. They'll try and convince us that we're doing too much, or that serving the Lord doesn't require that much commitment. They'll attempt to persuade us to compromise our integrity but don't give into their lies. People who even profess to be Christians will try with all their wit to wheedle you out of serving God with your whole heart. Resolve to go the hard way in. Purpose to live against the grain of worldliness keeping in mind these words: "Know ye not that the friendship of the world is enmity with God? Whosoever therefore will be a friend of the world is the enemy of God" (James 4:4).

Throughout the Old Testament, we read of kings that forsook the ways of the Lord and chose rather to follow in the way of disobedience – the way of worldliness. These were men who didn't respect the throne enough to approach it with reverence. Solomon could have taken his responsibility lightly like those men and, as a result, become a poor leader, but he didn't, at least not initially.

As a boy, he had no doubt observed David his father bear the burden of rulership. He had seen his father's successes and took note of his failures, and I'm sure it was the failures of his father that contributed to his desire for wisdom. He didn't want to repeat those same poor decisions.

This is how we must approach fatherhood! We have to go into it with a sober mind, understanding the gravity of our responsibility; we're raising lions! We're guiding our children into a life of spiritual fruitfulness. We're preparing them for life in the wild! It's a wide-open world out there, and if they haven't come to know the whisper of the Spirit of God, they will wander lost. How we lead today will determine how they lead tomorrow. We have to desire the wisdom that only comes from God if we're going to train up dark maned men in the way of fruitfulness. If we're to raise our daughters to know their value and how to identify a strong man as a potential husband, we must understand that they will look to us first. Wisdom will be needed if we're to raise up children who lock into hunger vision and pursue after the glory of God without hesitation. Wisdom will be needed if we're to raise men of risk who don't shy away from buffalo-sized rewards.

We must present to them the importance of going the hard way into every facet of life and discourage them from taking the easy way out. The way less traveled won't appeal to them if, when they search, our pawprints cannot be found. Wisdom is most effectively taught from the heart of personal experience.

If we're lacking in wisdom – which we all are as we measure ourselves against Christ – then God invites us to ask Him just as Solomon did:

If any of you lack wisdom, let him ask of God, that giveth to all men liberally, and upbraideth not; and it shall be given him.

JAMES 1:5

Notice the subject of the text: anyone who lacks wisdom. An acknowledgement of lack must first take place before God will supply His provision. If we're delusional in thinking we've arrived, God will not so much as look our way. His Word tells us that He resists the proud and gives grace to the humble (1 Peter 5:5). Humility must become our raiment if we're to receive the wisdom that God provides and effectively lead our families the hard way in.

It's brains over brawn with God. It's muscle memory over muscle with the Almighty. We can spend hours upon hours training our sons to be the best athletes they can be, or we can use that time to train them in the way of wisdom. Winning the golden gloves is a neat accomplishment, but I'd rather my son know how to hold his own in the ring of life than on Showtime. He's going to be faced with some opponents that can inflict more damage than a blackened eye or a bruised rib. Opponents like lust and pride are waiting; they don't wear gloves either. He won't have a thirty second rest between rounds. If he's not prepared, his opponent will overwhelm him with blows to his heart and mind, his knees will eventually give out, and he won't be able to stand as a man. If I haven't taken the time to train him, he won't stand a chance.

A Better Way

The memory is quite vague now, but I recall driving alone one day to some destination I can no longer recall. I was behind the wheel in traffic, and as usual, I took the opportunity to think on some things. This was during the time of my wife's second pregnancy, so we were expecting our first son. A scenario came to mind as I was maneuvering through traffic. I began to assess how I'd respond if my son ever came to me to tell me that he was being bullied. What would I say? What would be the godly way of judging and responding to such a situation? Would I go to the other young man and handle the situation myself? But if I did that, how would he learn to navigate his way out of future conflicts? I can't run to his rescue every time – can I? Would I tell him to fight back? I began to think hard about this, trying my best to reason out the wisest approach to such a common issue.

Drawing from past experience and cultural norms, I naturally thought the best approach would be to tell him to knuckle up and fight back. But that was a natural thought, and I've come to learn that natural thoughts often contradict the will of God. I reason, "Fighting back isn't what Jesus teaches through His Word." Now I'm beginning to notice the mind of the Spirit intercepting the mind of the flesh. Unsatisfied with the easy and most natural response, I begin to think there has to be a better way. As I thought on it more and as I applied my heart to wisdom, I heard the whisper of the Spirit of God tell me, "Teach him to reason." When I heard those four simple words, my thoughts calmed like the morning after an evening storm. All was quiet and gentle. It made perfect sense. It fit perfectly like the last piece of a puzzle. My mind was quiet as I thought upon the wisdom in that very simple phrase.

I was then reminded of a short account written by none other than King Solomon in the book of Ecclesiastes. When I thought on it, I began to understand the lesson God was teaching me, a lesson I would need to teach my son in due time: *Wisdom is better than strength.*

This wisdom have I seen also under the sun, and it seemed great unto me: There was a little city, and few men within it; and there came a great king against it, and besieged it, and built great bulwarks against it: Now there was found in it a poor wise man, and he by his wisdom delivered the city; yet no man remembered that poor wise man. Then said I, Wisdom is better than strength.

ECCLESIASTES 9:13-16

The memory of this account coupled with those four simple words, "Teach him to reason," was the answer my heart was searching for. If we're to prepare our sons for the challenges they will inevitably face in this life, we will need to impart godly wisdom into their hearts. Instead of teaching him to always resort to fighting, we will need to teach them as Christ teaches us – teach him to reason.

There are so many instances throughout the gospels where we see Jesus confronted by so-called bullies. There were men that were always trying to catch Him in His words. They strove against Him in everything because they refused to receive Him. They were so against Him and His ways that they, on several occasions, attempted to do Him harm:

But now ye seek to kill me, a man that hath told you the truth,
which I have heard of God: this did not Abraham.

JOHN 8:40

And the scribes and chief priests heard it, and sought how they
might destroy him: for they feared him, because all the people was
astonished at his doctrine.

MARK 11:18

Then the Pharisees went out, and held a council against him, how
they might destroy him.

MATTHEW 12:14

And all they in the synagogue, when they heard these things, were
filled with wrath, And rose up, and thrust him out of the city, and
led him unto the brow of the hill whereon their city was built, that
they might cast him down headlong. But he passing through the
midst of them went his way.

LUKE 4:28-30

Never once do we read of Jesus retaliating in violence. Never once did our Lord raise his hand to smite any of them. He never fought fire with fire. He used the sword of His mouth as weaponry against the attacks of his enemies, and when it was clear His words would be of no use, He simply walked away. He was showing us a better way. His example teaches us the way of the Spirit.

It's in Jesus that we find our example, and it's in Him that we find the answers to life's most complicated problems. It's through the life of Christ that we find the blueprint for training our sons in the way of righteousness, wisdom, and fruitfulness. Tradition may teach violence as a necessary evil, but the life of Christ teaches otherwise. As fathers, we must decide which side we're on. Either we agree with tradition or we agree with Jesus; there can be no mixing of the two.

Train Him in the Way

Our first priority as fathers should be to ensure we are actively impressing the gospel of Jesus Christ onto our sons. We must get it into their hearts early on if they're to have a fighting chance at life. The world's principles do not align with God's and neither does its ways, so we shouldn't align with the world. When we attempt to teach our sons the way of righteousness but neglect to disapprove of worldly customs and trends, it only causes confusion, which in turn creates in him a desire to align with the world. Mixture is not appealing to the soul that desires clarity; either give him black or give him white, for grey is too ambiguous a color for him to stand by.

This was the work of Christ in the disciples. He came to set things straight and clarify the ways of life and death for all men. He made it black and white for us. Jesus made it His priority to teach His disciples His ways, though it proved challenging indeed. We see throughout the gospels Jesus' commitment to teach them lessons they had never before been taught. We see His intent in tearing down their worldly mentality as He purposed to build in them a spiritual focus and a fortitude that would stand the test of time. His doctrine completely capsized everything they held as true. Everything they thought of as familiar and therefore fair was brought into question every time He opened His mouth to teach. The traditions of their fathers, the ways of the elders, and the customs of their culture were no longer viable excuses for living below God's true standard of righteousness – intimacy with Christ.

The Way of Righteousness

Right living is the anomaly in our generation. You'd be hard pressed trying to find a man that doesn't resemble the likeness of the world or reek of the stench of wickedness. You'd exhaust much of your energy searching for such a man that has not bowed his knee to the ways of ungodliness and perverseness. The Bible isn't exaggerating when it states, "They are all gone out of the way" (Romans 3:12). But which way is the way mentioned in the verse?

It refers to the way of righteousness, God's intended way of life for man. There is a standard of rightness that we must give heed to. There's a legitimate and proper way of living our lives that God has already prescribed as right no matter how much people of the world want to undermine its validity. The way of the Bible is still and will always be right. The gospel of Jesus Christ is still the only gospel that saves us from our sins and propels us into a fiery determination to live holy and separate from the world. He's still the only One we can look to for guidance in the way of righteousness for He Himself is our righteousness (1 Corinthians 1:30).

This is the doctrine we must teach our sons. This is the way we must lead them in – the way of righteousness.

The Way of Wisdom

On day zero of Air Assault School, we were required to negotiate a grueling obstacle course. One of the obstacles that day was a tower with three different phases. The first phase is what I want to focus on. It was a twenty-foot rope climb. Sounds simple enough. Just climb your way to the top and move on to the next phase. But before this obstacle was a 40-foot vertical tower climb. Once we completed the climb and descended, we were able to move on to the next obstacle. It wasn't as easy as that. A power leap followed by a push-up is how we moved to each obstacle. If the obstacle was forty, sixty, or one hundred meters away, we were leaping and pushing the entire distance. So, you can imagine how physically draining this would be by the time you reached your next obstacle.

Well, there we were at the twenty-foot rope climb and I began to notice a trend. A lot of the guys were using sheer muscle to pull themselves up and were struggling in the process, some even falling in exhaustion. Their upper bodies were already stressed from all the pushups they had to do to get there. Others relied upon technique, specifically what's referred to as the J-hook. This is a climbing technique where the climber hooks the rope with his feet while in mid-air and pinches it between his feet. It allows for him to secure himself to the rope while using minimum strength and energy. Climbers that used this technique fared better than those that relied upon their strength. They were able to reserve more energy to be used for the follow-on obstacles. It's a wise approach to negotiating an obstacle. It's literally brains over brawn.

How similar are our lives to this obstacle course? Some approach life head on and attempt to negotiate its obstacles by personal strength alone. We put confidence in our own abilities and our own ways of thinking until we realize through sheer exhaustion that our way doesn't work no matter how hard we try. We go as far and as high as we can until our strength fails, and we know what happens when strength is depleted while suspended on a rope – we fall! But it doesn't have to be that way with our sons.

The fear of the Lord is the beginning of wisdom: and the knowledge of the holy is understanding.

PROVERBS 9:10

We can take the wise approach to life and train our sons in the way of wisdom. Here we see that the fear or reverence of the Lord is where it all starts. Having in heart a deep-seated respect for the Word of God is the initial step to a lifelong journey of servitude to Him. The Psalmist wrote in Psalm 119:15, "I will meditate in thy precepts, and have respect unto thy ways."

We're the ones that God has entrusted to instill this reverence into their hearts. We're the ones that act as God's hands and feet as we lead our sons in the way of wisdom. We must lead as He would. We must teach as He would. We must chasten as He would. I think we get the picture.

Depth

A man that withholds his hand is often seen as weak in the world. If you're not ready to go blow for blow, then you're seen as a sissy. But when we apply wisdom, we understand that strength is not demonstrated in how quickly we're willing to trade blows but rather in our level of restraint; how many blows can you take without returning one? Whatever that number is, it is an accurate grade on your level of true strength. The true definition of strength is *the power to resist or endure; the capacity of an object or substance to withstand great force or pressure.*[15] It's the capacity to resist not the capacity to retaliate.

He that is slow to anger is better than the mighty; and he that ruleth his spirit than he that taketh a city.

PROVERBS 16:32

How long does it take to get your water boiling? How much heat must be applied for you to become beside yourself? Would you consider yourself slow to anger? Are you a man that rules your inner man? These are questions that not many men consider, yet so many men think themselves to be strong.

Guys hit the gym hard all winter in preparation for the summer. By the time spring rolls around and the weather shows even a slight tinge of warmth, they're bringing out the tank tops and quad high shorts. We want to be seen as strong because, on one hand, strength is attractive and, on the other, it compels others to follow us.

If I were to present to you a lineup of seven men, six of which appeared physically weak, and asked you to choose the man you'd follow into battle, who do you think you'd choose? Without any knowledge of any of their prior life experience or current skill sets, which of the seven would you be willing to risk your life with? It's not a trick question; most of us would choose the only man that appeared physically strong.

We have a good handle on what physical strength looks like, but when it comes to true strength, the strength of the inner man, we're scratching our heads in uncertainty.

We're unsure because we've been taught all our lives that a man is strong if he can bench press 225 pounds twenty times. You've got a solid guy if he can deadlift 400 pounds with ease. We've been brainwashed into thinking that the true measure of a man's strength is in what he's capable of doing as opposed to what he refuses not to do. Becoming a man of fruitfulness will require more restraint than capability. Becoming a dark maned male necessitates control.

God is not impressed with what we can do, though He can use our abilities for His glory. He delights in a man that is more concerned and captured by what God can do. He desires a man that'll withhold his hand and allow Him to fight all his battles. This is the sort of man we must be before the eyes of our children.

Our sons will have a difficult time coming to bear the black mane – a staple of internal power and strength – if we don't understand the necessity of self-control. It will be terribly challenging for him to understand the hidden value of wisdom if we only place precedence on physical strength. As men eventually, we learn to play on our strengths. If Junior's mind hasn't been infused with the wisdom found in God's Word, then he'll respond to conflict in the only way that comes natural to him. If we haven't lived out a life of wisdom before him, he'll respond as we would. The hearts of our sons are calling out to us saying:

Dad, I want to be a man someday.

I want to be a real man as I am intended.

I sometimes envision myself older and all I see is you.

Does that mean that I'm going to be like you when I grow up?

I want to be like you.

I want to be strong like you.

I want to bear my mane rightfully.

But I need you to show me how.

Dad, do you have the depth required to allow God to lead us?

Six

Territorial Trials

Be sober, be vigilant; because your adversary the devil, as a roaring lion, walketh about, seeking whom he may devour.

1 PETER 5:8

MY INTEREST IN LIONS, AS FAR AS I CAN RECOLLECT, came about the day I watched *Lion King* for the first time as a boy. As the movie played, I grew more and more intrigued by the regal appeal of Mufasa. I gravitated towards his poise, how he walked about the grasslands confidently, and it drew something within me. His capacity to be strong when necessary and yet soft and gentle with the pride was beautiful art in my eyes. He seemed to have mastered two great extremes within himself: one being his natural instinct to protect and defend his own and the other being his natural affection for the pride.

There was a greater representation being depicted. However, I was too young to understand what it was at the time. Unbeknown to me, I was beholding a good example of manhood. As I sat in front of that old block television with my small frame and wide eyes, something began to grow within me. A desire broke forth and emerged from the flesh of my heart. It was the desire to be a man who possessed those same qualities I saw in that beautiful creature, and though this was the beginning of a powerful emerge, it would be met with great adversity.

Fast forward some ten years later and I find myself seated in the back of an SUV in an alley under the cover of night. I carried a piece of steel in my right hand and wore a black bandanna over my face. What followed wasn't in any fashion pleasant. I was with some other guys preparing to break into a man's house and rob him for what we thought would be several pounds of marijuana. The driver gave us a stern warning, "Look, if he tries something, you have to shoot him!" I had never been so nervous in my life, but I was willing to set my nerves aside for a chance to demonstrate my level of loyalty.

In moments of reflection when I reminisce upon my path in life - where I've been, and what I've done – I sometimes cringe at what crosses my mind. I could have been someone far different than who I am today. I was very much a follower of the world, but God's grace preserved me and covered me even in my ignorance. But at 16 years of age, I had become someone far different than who I had originally desired to be. The desire to be a man of virtue was within me, but I had no idea how to live that out, so I settled for becoming someone less noble.

I believe all men desire to live an honorable life – a life that others would want to emulate – one that is marked by noble character and that is pleasing in the sight of the Lord. But I also believe that not every man knows how to live that out. *The Way of the Mane* is my manual to you.

But what happened to me? Where did that little wide-eyed boy go? How did I go from that innocent boy to such a cruel young man? In a word: influence. It was the influence of the world – my peers, the music, the movies, the TV shows, and my virtual and physical environment that led to my becoming a scruffy maned militant. I wanted everything the world had to offer, and it didn't matter to me how I got it.

Another Level of Absence

Samuel Osherson, a professor of psychology at the Fielding Graduate University, says, "If the father is not there to provide a confident, rich model of manhood, then the boy is left in a vulnerable position... We often misidentify our fathers, crippling our identities as men."[16]

As boys, we awake to life expecting leadership. We expect our fathers to teach, mentor, and guide us into manhood, but too often, we're confronted with crushed expectations. We awake and find the television sitting in place of him, the music pulsing in place of his voice, and evil associations taking the place of his company. We awake to fraudulent fathers.

I had a crippled identity. Though I was blessed to spend time with my father on the weekends, it was during the week that I was left in a vulnerable position. This same vulnerability has contributed greatly to the identity crisis we're seeing in many of our young people today. This reality is one of the main reasons behind my writing this book. We need to know who we are by God's design. We need our crippled identities to be fixed by the Great Physician.

As boys, we've been left to our own devices. We've been delivered into the hands of cruel company. I say "delivered" because that is exactly what happens as an inevitable result of an abandonment of the responsibility of fathering. When a man abandons his post, he is effectively delivering his children into the hands of thieves.

One of the results of my mother and father's divorce was that my father and I no longer shared the same living space. This matters primarily for two reasons: time and observation.

No one can argue against the fact that the home is the most significant source of influence. This is true primarily because home is where we spend majority of our time and where we discover our identities. We gradually come into an understanding of who we are through a continual observance of our mothers and fathers as they live out their distinctive roles within the family. My father's displacement meant our time spent together would be cut to less than a third of what it was before his departure. This resulted in the vacant role of "father" during the five days of the week that he wasn't present. This is another level of absence. Those days and that time matters. But culture has quickly identified weekend fathers as men who are present. If we're to be totally honest, that's not entirely true.

Presence has to do with physical placement in a specific space. If we're saying that fathers who are physically present with their children two days a week are present fathers, then what's to be said of those fathers who are there every day of the week? Do we identify them as being "very present"? The answer is no. The fact is that men who dwell with their children continually are present fathers, at least physically, while men who see their children intermittently are absent to a degree. My father was absent to a degree, and that degree impacted my life in a major way.

For the record, I'm not sharing this perspective on father absence to beat up on men who are or have had to father their children intermittently. I'm sharing this because it's important that we understand what it means to be present in its truest meaning. Presence has to do with physical placement. I understand the reality is that some relationships fail unintendedly often resulting in the displacement of fathers. If this sounds like you, then don't take this as me saying you're an ineffective father. I'm not saying that. I'm saying that you've been absent to a degree, and I want you to know that degrees matter. I'm also saying that if you're to maximize your influence over your children, it will require a lot of time and a lot of observation.

From the age of five onward, my father and I were no longer under the same roof, opening the same refrigerator, sprawled out on the same sofa, or sharing the same oxygen. He was no longer as physically present as he had been in the past. The dynamic of my home had changed drastically, and as a young boy, I had not the mind to understand and thereby bear the weight of the change. Immediately following his departure, I plunged into a sunken state of depression coupled with rage. His displacement created in me a storm of confusion that I was too young to clear up.

From then forward, mine and my father's relationship would be confined to segments of time. Our relationship was now required to develop within limited intervals of time, and I was to become a man in his stead void of the necessary time and observation I would need to get there. There are many men who share a similar background. Satan sees the absence of our fathers, to whatever degree they may be absent, and he makes it his business to capitalize on it.

Daily Patrol

---

*No man can enter into a strong man's house, and spoil his goods,
except he will first bind the strong man; and then he will spoil
his house.*

MARK 3:27

Here's a hypothetical question: If you were a thief who specialized in home invasion, and I presented to you three different homes, two having a present and armed father inside, which would you choose for your next job?

Think it over.

It's not a trick question. Most of us would choose the only house that lacked the muscle and steel. Now let's say that I present to you three different homes and, before you make your decision, I warn you that all of them have a present and armed father. Which would you choose?

Take a moment.

Again, I'm not trying to trip you up. Most of us would decide to look someplace else. This happens because testosterone is a terrible deterrent to thievery! In like manner, if dad isn't present both physically and spiritually, the thief will come and spoil the treasure of the hearts of the family. But when there's a father that's present and armed with the knowledge of Christ, who takes the security of his home serious from both a physical and spiritual perspective, Satan will have a hard time spoiling his home.

---

*The thief cometh not, but for to steal, and to kill, and to destroy:
I am come that they might have life, and that they might have it
more abundantly.*

JOHN 10:10

The thief mentioned in this text refers to Satan. He's on a mission to steal what we've worked so hard to instill in our children. Fruit such as that of the Spirit wrought in the hearts of your pride are like jewels of gold in the window of your home – they capture his attention. He's out and about searching for a pride that he can take over. He's actively looking for scruffy maned males who pose no threat to his intrusion. If you're not bearing a dark mane, if you're not actively patrolling your territory, and if you're not a present husband and father, you're risking the life of your pride.

Lions are known for being territorial creatures. In fact, they fight most intensely when defending their home. A typical pride of lions, consisting of a few males, several lionesses, and their cubs, can occupy several hundred miles of territory, and it's their daily discipline to patrol it, keeping watch for intruders. This responsibility falls on the shoulders of the males. Patrolling territory is incredibly important to the continued strength and protection of the pride, because lions not only have to protect their cubs from predators, like cheetahs or hyenas, but also from infanticidal male lions. These pride-less males roam about looking for prides of their own and will challenge any male they encounter in an attempt to dethrone him, massacre his seed, and steal his pride. If you're the head of a pride of your own, it's your most sacred duty to patrol your territory, otherwise you risk losing your pride and your life altogether.

In like manner, as husbands and fathers, we have an inherent responsibility to patrol our territory. We must purpose to keep watch daily, exercising a constant state of vigilance over what belongs to us. Our eyes must remain peeled and our heads on the swivel as we protect our own. We must always bear in mind the stark reality of an active adversary who desires, with a fiery heart, the lives of each member of our prides.

There will always be a rival by the name Satan that desires to disrupt the calmness of your abode. There will always be an enemy lurking on the outskirts who wishes to strip you of your possession. This isn't heaven! This is earth! We can't afford to forget that. It's not all peaches and rose pedals here. This is no cake walk. It's survival of the fittest! This is Satan's domain, and if we're to challenge his authority and effectively defend our territory, we will have to come under the leadership of Christ.

Be sober, be vigilant; because your adversary the devil, as a roaring lion, walketh about, seeking whom he may devour.

1 PETER 5:8

Lions are considered ambush predators. This means that their success in hunting or dethroning rival males depends greatly upon their ability to maintain the element of surprise. They spot their prey, close the distance, and aggressively attempt to subdue the animal before it realizes it's in danger. Much of their prey rely heavily upon their sense of awareness to spot danger, and their lives are often determined by their level of vigilance. Should an antelope become complacent and think himself free of the potential of danger, he would soon find himself locked within the jaws of a lion, kicking, squealing, and gasping for air! Likewise, we can never afford to let our guard down. I don't want to compare us to prey. However, if we're not focused and on guard, that's exactly what we will become.

We must resist the tendency to become complacent in our minds and never forget that there's a murderous lion bent on bringing an end to our reign as husbands and fathers. He's looking for scruffy-maned males that are spiritually unprepared and mentally unaware, males that pose no threat to his intrusion. It's your pride that he's after. It's your heritage that he's intent on stealing. We will need to be sober and vigilant if we're to maintain the security of our territory.

Be Sober

When instructing us to be wary of our adversary the devil, Peter first encourages sobriety. He says, "Be sober." I'm sure you may have immediately associated this word with alcohol or drugs, and that's good, because often when we hear of sobriety that's what we think of. We've been conditioned to associate this word with harmful substances, but the soberness that the Bible speaks of encompasses a wide range of things that could potentially alter our state of mind. If we're to secure our territory, we will have to understand what it means to be sober from a biblical perspective.

The word "sober," used in our referenced text, means *to be free from the influence of intoxicants* in the Greek translation.[17] It speaks to a clearness of mind. Before we can exercise the right level of vigilance toward our adversary, we must be in the right state of mind. I've never known a drunk to be a good night watchman. Our heads will need be free of mind-altering substances just as much as they do of mind-altering hindrances. Paul refers to these hindrances as weights in Hebrews 12:1.

While some men may struggle with alcoholism, there are others who aren't bothered by its allurement. This is why our heads must be free of both substances *and* hindrances. There are hazards that threaten our state of mind that many men think nothing of, such as pornography, excessive video gaming, excessive entertainment, ungodly music, evil associations, and offensive television shows. These hazards all have the potential of influencing the way we think, which over time, causes our minds to pass into a state of spiritual insobriety.

"I will behave myself wisely in a perfect way... I will walk within my house with a perfect heart."

PSALM 101:2

The world is full of spiritual intoxicants that can potentially alter our state of mind. From the moment you leave in the morning to go to work to the moment you turn the key in returning home, you've encountered a great number of spiritual hazards. As a Christian man, it can be challenging just making it back home with a clean heart. There's so much out there that draws our attention, such as overheard conversations which more often than not are ungodly, women dressed inappropriately and immodestly, advertisements designed to incite covetousness, and dare I mention the all too convenient smart phone!

There's enough temptation to go around which is why we should at a minimum purpose to ensure our homes are free of mind-altering hindrances. King David did just that! He purposed to ensure that the place where he would spend his down time was swept free of offences (a cause of stumbling). How else would he be able to say, "I will walk within my house with a perfect heart." He goes on to say in verse three, "I will set no wicked thing before mine eyes: I hate the work of them that turn aside; it shall not cleave to me." David was intentional about being spiritually sober. He was intentional about patrolling his territory and so should we.

Sweep the House

Of the many chores inherent in having a home, there's one I really enjoy doing. Sweeping is one of my favorite things to do around the house. When I have some spare time, it's not uncommon for me to pick up the broom and start sweeping. I know that I enjoy it, because if I see some crumbs on the floor that my children may have left after eating a snack, I'll find myself sweeping the whole house as opposed to just that area of the kitchen floor. My mother kept a pristine house, and I know for a fact that her routine cleaning left a lasting impression on me. When I shared my enjoyment of sweeping with my father, he said that for him it was ironing his clothes; maybe it's something different for you.

I enjoy sweeping really for one reason: I appreciate a floor free of debris. There's nothing quite like walking around your house barefoot and noticing that after 10 minutes nothing has clung to your soles! In like manner, as the head of my house and spiritual leader of my family, I purpose to sweep the place free of spiritual debris. I realize that it's my responsibility to ensure that nothing has infringed upon my territory. It's important to me to ensure that both my and my family's spiritual sobriety are intact and that our home isn't a hub for housing spiritual intoxicants like the ones I mentioned earlier. Instead, our sweet abode must be that of a place fit to encourage sober thought – a place that's conducive to spiritual sobriety.

We want our children growing up in a home free of worldly influence, and I realize that it's up to me to ensure it happens. I take my and my family's service to God and representation of Him serious, more serious than anything else. But my leadership style is not a dictatorship. My wife and children understand the reason why we exercise discretion. They too are serious about their testimony for Christ, and when this is the resolve and shared passion of the family, your territory will remain secure. However, there are those who will try to convince us that being a Christian doesn't require all that effort. They say that God's not concerned with what we watch, what we listen to, the company we keep, or what we wear.

We're not buying it!

These men are the same men who are, from a spiritual perspective, void of fruit. They are men who don't yield their fruit in their season because they've chosen to walk in the counsel of the ungodly, stand in the way of sinners, and sit in the seat of the scornful (Psalm 1:1). They are no different than dead trees because they've chosen to establish roots with the ungodly. They are males who suffer from a bad case of manelessness. Such men possess hearts given over to worldliness and are too blind to see that their ways do not align with God's. When confronted by these mane-less males, who speak more than they listen, remember to exercise your sixth sense and avoid them (Titus 3:9).

We want to resemble God more than we resemble the world. Daily priorities such as reading God's Word and meditating upon what we read, praying, frequenting the house of God, fellowshipping with the saints, and spending quality time together will make the difference in my and your children's lives. These disciplines are the cobblestones that lead us to a victorious Christian life.

A Clean House Encourages a Clean House

I believe all Christians desire to lead holy lives marked by a reverence and obedience to God's Word. But when we're attempting to live holy while harboring spiritual intoxicants in our homes our progress is frustrated.

Remember the definition of sober? It's *to be free from the influence of intoxicants.* Whether we realize it or not, we choose what we allow to influence our minds. When we decide to pick up a title to read, or to watch our favorite series online, or to hang around a certain person or group of persons, we're deciding to be influenced. We're allowing some external source to gain entrance into our minds which will, in turn, affect our thought life, and we know where thoughts lead. Influences can either be for the better or worsening of our spiritual sobriety.

One man put it this way, "The authors you read, the artist you listen to, and the actors you watch are all your buddies. They're people that you like to hang out with. The amount of time you spend with them will affect the amount of influence they'll have in your life." Steve Farrar, author of *Point Man*, puts it simply when he says, "Less time equals less influence, and more time equals more influence."[18] It's a simple formula, but it's true, nonetheless.

We should starve our fleshly desires for things we know will hinder our relationship with God and aggressively feed our desire for holiness (Romans 13:14). Monitoring what's being pumped into your and your family's minds is vitally important. The safekeeping of your home from ungodly influences will foster an environment where you and your family can grow spiritually – one where you and your family will want to grow spiritually!

Once we've made a conscious decision to rid our homes of spiritual intoxicants, God will grab His luggage full of wonderful, life changing things and will ask to come in. It's always been this way with God. He's always required unoccupied space for Himself in the hearts of His people (Matthew 22:37). He's always required an invitation, and a great way of bidding God's presence is ridding our lives of things He would find offensive. Knowing this should propel us into action ensuring our homes are habitats that encourage holiness.

Be Vigilant

Once we've purposed to rid our lives of spiritual intoxicants and we're moving in a direction of spiritual sobriety, we're now able to exercise the proper level of vigilance toward our adversary. Keeping watch does no good if you don't know what you're looking for. Having a sober mind that's been washed by the Word of God is what enables us to positively identify our adversary before he's gotten too close, before he's gained too great an advantage.

In the Greek, vigilance means *to keep awake* or *to be watchful*.[19] Peter was cautioning us to keep our spiritual eyes open and our spiritual senses keen. I find it interesting how Peter chose to describe Satan in 1 Peter 5:8. He depicts him "as a roaring lion." There's some significance in that description that we should look further into.

Roaring is one of the characteristics attributed most to the male lion. If you were to ask a small child to act like a lion, chances are they'd probably ball their face up in a snarling way, bend their fingers as if to show claws, and give their best roar. We know that lions roar, but have you ever wondered why they roar? What's the significance behind their aggressive expression? Well, to put it simply, lions roar primarily to express dominance over their territory.

It's like being a soldier on guard duty in a combat zone. If someone approaches the perimeter of your compound too closely, dependent upon your rules of engagement, you're typically expected to follow the simple guideline: shout, show, shoot! According to this guideline, soldiers shout at potential intruders, and if that doesn't work, they raise the muzzle of their rifle in the trespassers direction as a deterrent. Finally, if all else fails, the trigger is to be squeezed, forcing the threat to cease his unlawful progression forward.

In like manner, lions roar as a hard deterrent. If he roars, he's sending a message to all would-be trespassers, saying, "This is my domain; leave now or challenge me if you dare."

These roars can reach an incredible 114 decibels, about 25 times louder than a gas operated lawnmower. That's loud! It's so loud that it can be heard up to five miles away. So, when Peter describes Satan as a roaring lion, he's telling us that Satan is walking about actively expressing his dominance over this world. He's crying out, "This is my domain; leave now or challenge me if you dare!" He's territorial in every sense of the meaning. He's bent on conquering every facet of your and your family's minds, and he will stop at nothing to ensure he accomplishes that end.

Deciding to trek along *The Way of The Mane* is our way of letting him know that we're not cowering in fear at his threats any longer. Are you prepared to challenge the authority of Satan? If Satan showed up at your front door today, what would you do? Would you invite Him in? What if he forced himself in? Would you be strong enough to resist him? I can tell you that, without the power of God, you will fail in your attempts to protect your territory from the power of the enemy. You must bear in mind that your territory was his to begin with. The Bible tells us that we are born in sin. We also know that this world is pitifully subjected to the power and influence of Satan. It's not until we accept the Lord Jesus into our hearts and begin to follow Christ that we are no longer subjected to Satan's power (Colossians 1:13).

Wherein in time past ye walked according to the course of this world, according to the prince of the power of the air, the spirit that now worketh in the children of disobedience.

EPHESIANS 2:2

Satan is known as the prince of the power of the air. This means that he has the authority to exercise great influence over this present world. Like many people you may know, we were under this evil influence prior to our coming to know Christ. We lived according to our fleshly desires, pursued after ungodly interests, and took pleasure in sin. Our territory was completely under his rulership. We were completely ruled by him and were by nature the children of Satan, the children of disobedience.

Post-salvation, everything changed. The victory that Jesus won in dying and rising again is what enables us to be in this world but not of it. His victory is our confidence. His victory is why we no longer tremble at the roar of Satan when we hear it.

If you listen with your spiritual ears, you'd have no problem hearing the roar of Satan in day-to-day life. I hear him in the office, boasting with foul language through untamed tongues. I hear his roar faintly through the headphones of other men as I share space in the gym. His roar can be heard through secular music and television shows. His boastful cry can be perceived in the voice of all who oppose the gospel and speak proudly of the ways of darkness and perverseness. If you listen close enough, you will have no trouble hearing Satan. If we're not careful and purposeful in our effort to live for God, we might even hear him out of our own mouths.

Remember when Peter rebuked Jesus?

It happened around the time that Jesus began to disclose more information regarding His death and resurrection to His disciples. Peter, upon hearing that Jesus would be killed said what any carnally-minded man would say to his friend. The Bible says in Matthew 16:22, "Then Peter took him, and began to rebuke him, saying, Be it far from thee, Lord: this shall not be unto thee." Seems like Peter was being a friend to Jesus. It seems that Peter did the right thing in wanting to protect his Lord from the threats of His foes. But we know that Peter's response was earthly and totally contradicted the will of God. We learn by Jesus' response to Peter's rebuke to be watchful, guarding our hearts with all diligence to ensure that Satan doesn't gain an advantage within us. We learn that though we follow Jesus we can never get so lax that we forget to learn from Him.

But he turned, and said unto Peter, Get thee behind me, Satan: thou art an offense unto me: for thou savourest not the things that be of God, but those that be of men.

MATTHEW 16:23

Notice how Jesus checks Satan immediately. Jesus was on guard, actively patrolling His territory. Those men were His disciples, they were His students, and the will of God was His to fulfill. In like manner, our children are our own, our families belong to us, and the call of God upon our lives is ours to fulfill. God has entrusted them under our care. We must be actively vigilant. We must give good attention to the encroachment of the enemy. We must keep our minds focused on the will of God for us and our families. Jesus' sensitivity to the will of God enabled Him to always detect the voice of the roar of the enemy. Peter didn't realize it then, but he had unintentionally permitted the roar of Satan to hijack his tongue, and if we're not vigilant, it can happen to us just the same.

Go in Anyway

I don't know where this chapter finds you. Maybe you're already regularly patrolling your territory. Maybe you're already exercising vigilance and doing everything necessary to secure what belongs to you. But maybe you're not. Maybe you've neglected this vital responsibility, and it's beginning to show. Maybe your pride is suffering from territorial trials. Maybe, due to your lack of vigilance, you've allowed the enemy to infringe upon your territory.

This usually manifests itself in the unfamiliarity of our children, our wives, and even ourselves. We wonder when considering the behavior of our children, "When did she start talking that way?" Or we may think, "When did he become so cold?" The influence of the world begins to manifest itself through the breakdown of morals and ethics within the family. When we've allowed Satan to gain access to our prides, he begins to go to work. Remember, his intentions are to dethrone you, massacre your seed, and ultimately steal your pride. When we find ourselves perplexed at the condition of our homes, we should retrace our steps. When our house is not a home and everyone is to themselves in their own little world, we must stop to consider what's happened. When we and our families resemble worldliness and we find that we are more like the world than we are of God, we need to pause in place.

Realizing the effects of shirking our patrolling duty in involving ourselves in every facet of the family can be overwhelming for any mane-bearer. I know it was for me. I remember my and my family's life just being so contrary to fundamental biblical teachings. I remember feeling so weighed down by my own sin and by an ever-present thought that would haunt my spirit, a thought I just couldn't shake no matter what I did. It was a condemning thought that said, "You're failing in leading your family," and it was true.

I couldn't run away from it, and I felt that I couldn't change and be the man that they needed and that God required. From my perspective, I had allowed too much time to pass in neglecting my patrolling duty. By this time, I'm sure Satan or one of his goons was sitting on my couch with his feet propped up on my table laughing as my house was in turmoil. The thought of regaining my territory would overwhelm me. Is it possible? How will my wife ever be vulnerable with me again? My daughter needed me to be soft and gentle, but I had always been hard and rough with her. How will we ever have that strong bond and relationship that I know she needs? I felt utterly defeated, and I'm sure that's exactly how the enemy wanted me to feel. He was almost successful in dethroning me as the head of my family.

Karen McComb, a professor of animal behavior and cognition at the University of Sussex, measured the responses of female lions to recorded roars of unfamiliar females. She discovered that female lions typically prefer to confront invading females when the odds are ever in their favor. She found that they're more confident in facing intruding females when they have an advantage in numbers by at least two to one.

Jon Grinnell, a biology professor at Gustavus Adolphus College, found an opposite sense of "numeracy" in males. When given the same scenario, the male lions would sometimes confront intruders even if they were outnumbered three to one.[20]

That's bold!

But it shouldn't be surprising to us. We know that territory is everything to a mane-bearer. His territory provides a refuge and sense of safety for the members of his pride, so if it's taken, he knows he must do everything in his power to try and regain control. It's so important to him that he's willing to confront several other males just as strong as him by himself. It's a defensive front that has defeat written all over it, but that's okay, because dark maned males are willing to die for what belongs to them!

If you're feeling outnumbered and overwhelmed because you've unintentionally allowed the enemy inside of your territory, take heart! If you sense that things have gotten out of hand in your home and it seems that it'll be impossible to regain control, look alive! As a brother who's been in a similar scenario, I encourage you to go in anyways! The roar of the enemy will only get louder the more we try and ignore him. He must be confronted! Even if it seems that everyone is against you and there is no one to support you in your effort to take back your territory, go in anyway!

Initially, it may seem that you're alone, and you may wonder whether the risk is worth the rewards. When you feel tempted to allow things to continue as they are, remember that God is in risk, and that if you go in faith, He will go with you. Greater is He that is in you than he that is in your territory.

Ha! I like that!

Muster up the courage to regain your territory and fight for your pride! Fight for the heart of your wife and children! Fight for holiness! Fight for righteousness! Fight for your heritage! Fight for your testimony!

Get back to praying daily and reading your Bible. Don't just read it, eat it! Look at the words of Scripture as meat for your soul. Make it a priority to be in God's house and settle it in your heart. Migrate your way to the confluence! Get to the river and defend it with your life. When Satan roars, don't be afraid to roar back. Roar over your pride. Roar over your territory.

Seven

Cleave To What Is Good

Abhor that which is evil; cleave to that which is good.

ROMANS 12:9

A S MANE-BEARERS THE RESPONSIBILITY OF THE PRIDE falls upon our shoulders. God doesn't give us higher levels of testosterone and equip us with a stronger anatomy for us to follow the leadership of our wives – that goes against nature. We're the ones in the cockpit piloting as He would have us. We're the ones designated as foreman with clipboard in hand, ensuring we're building according to the specs of Scripture. When it's all said and done, it's the mane-bearer that must give account for the way he leads his pride, because it's the mane-bearer that God created for leadership.

But I would have you know, that the head of every man is Christ; and the head of the woman is the man; and the head of Christ is God.

1 CORINTHIANS 11:3

This text clearly identifies the man, you and I, as the head of our wives, but what does it mean to be the head. In simple terms, it means that we're the ones designated by God to lead. As Christ, our Head, leads us, we lead our wives and children. Think of it from an anatomical perspective. Nothing happens within the confines of our mortal bodies until our brains or our heads send messages through electrical neurons to the rest of the body. This means that your left to right eye motion as you read this chapter is only happening because your brain is communicating with the nerves in your eyes. Any action taken by the body traces back to that initial signal sent from the brain; it traces back to the leadership of the mind.

It's no different with leading a family. We're sending signals every day to our wives and children. Our actions and inactions greatly influence how our wives and children will respond to life and how they'll serve the Lord. We are their examples just as Christ is our example. They follow us as we follow Him. As the head, we send signals to them in how we respond to pressure and anxiety. Signals are sent in how we communicate and interact with them and others, where and with whom we spend our time, and essentially how we live our day-to-day lives. We send signals to them when we prioritize personal and family time with God. They begin to reason, "Daddy sees God as important, so I should too." But it works the same in the inverse. If we're not committed to a life of godliness, it's likely our families won't commit either. We set the standard for our homes by our example and every sent signal will eventually produce a response.

I recently learned of a profound statistic with regard to a man's influence over his family that fits perfectly with what we're discussing. An article published by *Polly House* back in 2003 states, "If a child is the first person in a household to become a Christian, there is a 3.5 percent probability everyone else in the household will follow. If the mother is the first to become a Christian, there is a 17 percent probability everyone else in the household will follow. But if the father is first, there is a 93 percent probability everyone else in the household will follow." The author continues, "We don't have to have statistics to tell us this is true. There is something in the hardwiring of creation that naturally causes wives and children to look to husbands and fathers to lead out."[21]

We should give serious thought to how we intend to lead our families because it matters. One day, if they haven't already, your children will leave and go off into an open world. What you instill in them now will make the difference in their lives; it will greatly influence their path in life.

Dig Deep

In chapter six, "Territorial Trials," we talked about the importance of regaining lost territory. We determined within our hearts that even if the odds are stacked against us and we're seemingly outnumbered, we're going in anyway. Come hell or high water, we're going to regain what's rightfully ours. While this is a great start, I'd be remiss if I didn't tell you that it takes more than a spark to keep the fire burning. It takes more than an initial stride and energy to finish a marathon. It takes more than sheer desire and motivation to continue and see things through. It takes heart! It takes a heart with an irreversible agenda, an unquenchable passion, and an unwavering focus to recapture the heart of the pride. It takes a heart that will stop at nothing until its desire is fulfilled. It takes heart to win hearts.

If we're truly intentional about being mane-bearers fit to recapture the hearts of our pride, we will have to prepare our minds for the long haul. We will have to accept that things may get worse before they get better. We can't be afraid of enduring some scars in the process. Having the courage of a lion doesn't mean that we're immune to the fight we will encounter, and make no mistake about it, Satan will fight you every step of the way. Lions are seen through our human lens as courageous because they possess the heart to fight, and they don't shy away from the potential of pain. We must remember that Satan is territorial and that once he's seized upon an area he intends to keep it forever. But mane-bearers don't shy away from a fight! Black maned males welcome adversity with open arms and a smile on their faces. If you've lost territory, I'm telling you plainly, there will be adversity in your attempt to regain control. Don't allow the thought of the work that lies ahead to discourage you from moving forward and going in anyway. Yes, there will be push back, but know that it's in our response to adversity that we find our measure. Take heart and fight!

Not everyone will be convinced of the change that's occurred in your heart. They may have grown accustomed to the old mangy maned fella you once were, so when it seems that you're catching friction, take heart, grit your teeth, and remain consistent. We will have to be patient and show forth a consistency of character as we await God's timing. We must trust that God is working in us and through us to bring about the change that is needed in us and in our pride.

Prayer will have to be non-negotiable. Reading our Bibles and taking time to meditate on Scripture will have to become a normal part of our day. Getting locked into a Bi-ble-believing church will need to be a highlighted portion of your action plan. Remember the confluence!

One of the more fascinating features of the male lion apart from his mane are his claws. Armed with eighteen impressive rump-snatching daggers, five on each paw in the front, and four on each paw in the rear, they make good use of them when capturing their prey. In fact, without their claws, lions would have little to no success in taking down prey and defending themselves and their prides against intruding males. It's a weapon they can't go without.

If you've ever streamed a video of a pride of lions hunting buffalo, you know exactly what I'm talking about. It usually looks something like a herd of buffalo scattering desperately as one or two males trot around looking for the one they intend to go for. Once they make their decision and they set their focus on the one they want, they go for it!

Immediately, they rush him from different angles causing the beast to enter into a state of intense confusion and panic. If he goes left, there's a snarled-faced lion there. If he goes right, there's another. If he decides to flee to the rear, there they are again. He finds himself franticly moving in circles, exhausting loads and loads of energy while going nowhere. They corner him quickly, cutting off all routes of evasion, and eventually when the timing is right, one of the males will approach the animal from its rear, raise himself up, unsheathe his claws and clamp down! It's like that scene out of *Lion King* when Scar is overlooking Mufasa as he hangs from a cliff begging his ill-hearted brother to save him. Scar responds by sinking his claws into the paws of Mufasa causing Mufasa to screech in agony. Though fictional, this is an accurate depiction of what it must feel like to be on the receiving end of ten razor sharp claws all at once.

At this stage of the hunt, the male hanging on to the rump of the buffalo plays a significant role. The weight of his 350 to 500-pound frame slows the beast and causes him to reach exhaustion at an accelerated rate. The lion's piercing claws create a painful irritation in the buffalo's mind, causing him to move hastily and make bad decisions. The longer the lion cleaves to the buffalo the greater the pride's chances of bringing him down. He can't let go!

Capturing the hearts of the members of your pride is a buffalo-sized reward, and like hunting buffalo, it'll require us to dig deep and hang on for the ride of our lives. We will need to sink our spiritual claws into what is good and resolve in our minds never to let go no matter what happens.

The Good of God's Word

One of the many things I love about the Bible is that God thought it necessary to showcase so many men just like you and me. I appreciate the wisdom, encouragement, and insight we gather from reading into the lives of these men. We have the opportunity to learn from their poor decisions so as not to repeat them, but we can also learn from their successes as encouragement for how we should go about our lives serving the Lord.

For whatsoever things were written aforetime were written for our learning, that we through patience and comfort of the scriptures might have hope.

ROMANS 15:4

God has given us His Word that we might learn from the accounts that are scribed within and go on to live lives that glorify Him. We are never without examples. We may not have had the best of role models when we were growing up, but we can't overlook the fact that God has provided us many men as examples and models of godliness. He's given us men whose lives read more like fiction than fact, when in fact, they were just ordinary men who realized they had an extraordinary calling upon their lives.

One such is a man who went by the name Eleazar. In the Hebrew tongue, his name means *God helps* – a fitting name for a man who relied upon the help of God in battle.[22] He was one of King David's mighty men and like all thirty-seven of David's men, he earned his title in heroic fashion. Of the thirty-seven mighty men, Eleazar was ranked only second to Adino, a man that managed to defend himself against eight hundred enemy soldiers using only his spear and expertise. What sort of heart must a man have to fight against eight hundred foes and walk away with his life?

To be named among David's mighty men, one had to possess a heart of courage and loyalty, but to be named among the chief three, one had to have a heart of extraordinary courage and loyalty. Eleazar was cut from the same cloth as Adino. He was one of the three that overheard David when he made mention of the well of Bethlehem in the cave of Adullam. David and his men were under siege by the garrisons of the Philistines when the king began to long for a drink of water.

And David was then in an hold, and the garrison of the Philistines was then in Beth-lehem. And David longed, and said, Oh that one would give me drink of the water of the well of Beth-lehem, which is by the gate!

2 SAMUEL 23:14-15

Those words of the king fell upon the ears of three intensely loyal men, and it moved them into action. The Bible states in the next verse of that same chapter that these men, Eleazar included, broke through the host of the Philistines and took the water from the well that their king desired. It doesn't say that they politely asked for a courtesy cup of Bethlehem's finest spray. It says that they took it! Though the Philistines had taken Bethlehem as their territory, it didn't change the fact that the well belonged to David and his men. It was theirs, and because it was theirs, they went and took it back.

Sound familiar?

In the fight to regain lost territory, we don't ask politely if we can have our things back. In fact, we don't ask at all! Your pride is yours and yours alone. If Satan has even the slightest touch of influence over what belongs to you, it's past time to lace up your boots, grab your helmet and sword, and contend for the hearts of your pride.

These men risked their lives to quench the thirst of their king. What fierce loyalty! What are you willing to risk in order to win the hearts of your wife and children? What are you willing to lose that you might gain their hearts and ultimately influence them to serve the Lord?

Eleazar and his comrades were lionhearted men in every sense of the word. Eleazar was willing to risk it all because he was loyal to the desire of his king. He wanted what His king wanted and was willing to risk everything to capture it. We, like Eleazar, must be loyal to our King, the Lord Jesus. We must desire what He desires and be willing to capture those desires of His, which include influencing our prides in the way of righteousness. Eleazar was a man of war, which is why I've chosen to highlight him as a role model for us to emulate.

We too must become men of war, capable of battling and holding our own in the spiritual convoy of regaining lost territory. As I've stated earlier, Satan will not just hand over what he's taken from us. We will have to go in understanding that a fight awaits us. We must be prepared to tussle and contend for the hearts of every member of our pride.

I say we have to be prepared, because battles are often long and drawn out. In natural warfare, especially at the onset, it can take quite some time to gain even the smallest amount of ground against the enemy. Armies are often forced to bunker down and inch their way forward into the enemy's ground while enduring a hail of firepower. This methodical progression is only achieved when unit commanders and their troops have prepared for the long haul through rigorous training and are determined to advance no matter what. Our man Eleazar was that kind of solider – trained and determined.

And after him was Eleazar the son of Dodo the Ahohite, one of the three mighty men with David, when they defied the Philistines that were there gathered to battle, and the men of Israel were gone away:

2 SAMUEL 23:9

Here we find a chronicle of David and his three mighty men when they were alone fighting for their lives against a host of Philistine soldiers. The Bible tells us that the men of Israel were gone away in verse nine and goes on to say in the latter part of verse ten that they only returned to take of the spoils that David and his men had secured through fierce fighting. They were alone. This meant that each man had to hold his own weight and fight his own fight. They were outnumbered, and probably outsized as the Philistines were known to breed men of extraordinary stature. But though they may have been outnumbered and outsized, they were far from outmatched. Eleazar may have been outnumbered in terms of personnel strength, but when we look outside the box, we find that he actually had the advantage.

He arose, and smote the Philistines until his hand was weary, and his hand clave unto the sword...

2 SAMUEL 23:10

Heart and Sword

His advantage was that he had a heart that was affixed to his sword. He was a warrior, and like any career combatant, his sword meant everything to him; it was his shield and protection that kept him safe from the attacks of his enemies. It was his primary means of defense, so you can imagine how skillful he must've become in its use.

I'm reminded of how as soldiers we're religiously trained to maintain positive accountability of our rifles. In basic training, we gave names to them, and drill sergeants often reinforced the notion that our M16s were our new wives — our enlistment contracts being the binding agreement that would keep us together. Though humorous, I find some legitimacy in the practice, nonetheless. I distinctively recall the jaw-dropping moments when soldiers would accidentally drop their rifles on the pavement. The sound of metal hitting hard stone would reverberate, bringing with it utter silence. It was as if the world stood still for a moment as each soldier awaited the all too familiar phrase from the drill instructor, "Down with it!" One man's negligence brought pain and sweat to an entire company of troops.

During deployments, our rifles are the one thing that stays by our side every moment of every day. When we rise in the morning, it's there next to us by our cots. When we go to brush our teeth and wash our faces, it's there slung across our chests. In the chow hall, in the laundry room, on the toilet, and on duty, it's there with us, and we know why. Like Eleazar, it's our primary means of defense.

I like how the Bible says that Eleazar fought until his hand was weary. This meant that he was using his sword to his fullest extent. He was actively fighting his enemy. He was holding his ground.

Developing a healthy relationship with your wife and children will require great effort, and there may be days when you want to just throw in the towel. There may be days when you feel that it's all for naught, that all the effort and energy you're exhausting are in vain. But when you feel the urge to quit, remember Eleazar. Consider how he may have felt in the battle he was faced with. He may have been tempted to quit as well. Maybe the temptation to quit came to his mind. Maybe he began to wonder when, if ever, the enemy would cease their assault. Maybe he thought, "How many more do I have to fight off?" Maybe he was tempted to feel self-pity when he felt his hand go numb. Regardless of how he may have felt and how many temptations may have come his way, we see his response. The Bible says that "his hand clave unto the sword," and it's in his response to adversity that we find his measure.

In simple terms, Eleazar clave unto what was good. He held on to the only thing that could deliver him from the brutal attacks of his enemy – he held on to his sword. When his flesh began to lose hold, it was his heart that held on and tightened his grip. His heart and his sword were one!

And take the helmet of salvation, and the sword of the Spirit,
which is the word of God.

EPHESIANS 6:17

Like Eleazar, we too have need of a sword as accompaniment into the dangers of infringing upon stolen ground. God's Word is what we must cleave to if we have any hope of leading our prides in righteousness and influencing not only our children but also generations to come after them. Eleazar was loyal to the sword, and we see the extent of his loyalty in his unwillingness to quit. His devotion to what was good enabled him to push pass the point of weariness. Can we say that we're as loyal to God and His Word as Eleazar was to his sword? Is it God that we cleave to when our strength is failing and our hearts are on the verge of giving in? If the answer is no, use the realization of this self-assessment as fuel to get you going on the right track.

*My flesh and my heart faileth: but God is the strength of my heart,
and my portion forever.*

PSALM 73:26

Weariness is just a natural byproduct of life; no one is above it. There was a guy in my unit when I was stationed in South Korea that would always say, "I don't get tired!", whenever we would do physical training. Sweating bullets and clearly out of breath, he would yell it to the top of his lungs, but the evidence always proved otherwise. His body was testifying against him. I'm sure he was just trying to motivate himself to push a little further, but for some reason, he saw weariness as a sign of weakness, but that's not the case. Growing tired doesn't mean you're weak; it just means you're human. It's in how we respond to weariness that we find our strength. Do we continue and push through it even though everything in us is telling us to quit, or do we just let go?

The extent of our strength cannot be accurately assessed on a good day; we find our truest measure of strength on our worst day. Strength is a choice just like everything else in life. We choose to be strong just like we choose to give up. Strength is looking down at your hand in a moment of realization when you sense that it stopped working but deciding to fight anyway. Strength is riding the hind parts of a massive buffalo and refusing to let go until you've won the victory. Strength, my friend, is digging deep into what is good and refusing to let go.

You see, if we haven't sunken our claws into what is good, we will eventually lose our hold on the buffalo we intend to take down. Sink your spiritual claws into the Word of God, knowing that the rewards that lie within are greater, much better, and more bountiful than you can imagine.

The Good of a Godly Wife

When considering things worth holding on to in our effort to secure the pride, we must consider our wives. Prides aren't run effectively by males alone. The lioness does most of the hunting and cares for the young. Realizing the great value that our wives add to our lives will encourage us to cleave unto them and the relationship when things are rocky.

Therefore shall a man leave his father and his mother, and shall cleave unto his wife: and the two shall be one flesh.

GENESIS 2:24

Prior to my wife and I marrying, I like to say that my life in general was easy going. I was a young soldier just beginning my career in the Army, so a lot of my time was spent either in the gym or in my barracks' room, watching the original *Star Trek* series. In fact, my lunchtime routine consisted of sherbet ice cream and a quick watch of Spock and Kirk navigate the complexities of the universe. Yeah, I know I was a strange guy, but as the saying goes, to each his own.

I was spending a lot of time alone. In my own estimate, I esteemed myself as self-controlled and disciplined, but this was because my personal life involved only myself. It's easy to view yourself in a pleasant light when you haven't been tested. I've always kept a small circle, and when I left for boot camp, my circle became a dot, so there was little opportunity for true confrontation. I wasn't socially active. Sure, I'd get into squabbles with the soldiers in my unit but that was easy to manage. Duty was duty and that was it. I'm talking about the sort of skirmishes that strike the heart and reveals things about everyone involved – personal matters. I hadn't yet experienced this enough to accurately gain an assessment of myself – a true estimate of me.

I often refer to myself at this stage in my life as a white wall. My life was simple, seemingly without fray and easily manageable. I presented myself as model soldier. I was rough, rigid, and resilient when it came to Army life, but that all changed April 23rd, 2014! This was the day my wife and I exchanged vows – the day I met my true self. I soon realized that while I may have been an efficient soldier, I was an inefficient man and husband.

We started our marital journey alone in the Midwest with no friends or family nearby. It was just me and her every day, and we preferred it that way. I remember the first year being such a trial. She was different. Not different from what I knew her to be, but just different than me. I wanted everything dress-right-dress, while she didn't mind a little disorganization. I had a certain way to clean the floor after a juice spill, and she had hers. I distinctively remember frustratedly expressing to my new beautiful bride after a spill in the kitchen, "You have to use both soap and water or else the floor will be sticky!" She couldn't understand why I would be so upset at something so insignificant. The point I'm trying to make is that I was one way, and well, she was another. She was different.

Often, we downplay our differences and uplay the things we have in common. But in my experience, though I didn't see it then, I now realize that it's been our differences that has contributed greatly to our relationship and union. I was a dry white wall and to me she was colorful wet paint. At the time, I saw her wet paint as a great contrast and hindrance to my preferred simple state. She was messing everything up. However, in hindsight, I see very clearly that her arrayment of color was exactly what I needed in my life. I needed her to disrupt some things. I needed her to splash some color in my life.

Whoso findeth a wife findeth a good thing, and obtaineth favour of the Lord.

PROVERBS 18:22

My life changed completely when I found my wife. I had never been challenged the way that our relationship and union has challenged me. This was the first time I had allowed someone in close. It was the first time in all my life I opened my heart up to another person. Now that I think of it, I was much like the beast in Disney's classic, *Beauty and the Beast.* I had grown accustomed to being on my own. The vines had grown over the fencing used to keep others at bay. The silence of my chambers had become my music, and I was too stubborn to welcome change. I guess I thought I'd gain a wife and lose nothing, but it was needful for me to lose some things. My ways weren't perfect, and there were areas within myself that needed to die off.

This good thing that I had found was good indeed! She was the very one that brought about my awareness of certain inhibitions that once lay dormant within me. It was her vibrant paint that revealed the small yet significant hidden holes in my life. It was this good thing that God used to push some bad things out of me and work some good things in me, and I'm sure He's doing the same thing for you in your marriage.

You see, our wives are good for us. It's the design of God that they support and aid us in all we do. We can't lead our prides without them. The relationship is made difficult when we purpose to do everything on our own and in our own way. It took me a long time to accept that my wife is my helper. My stubbornness and unwillingness to allow her to aid me over the course of time caused me to inevitably view her as some sort of enemy of mine. Her offered assistance became nothing more than a redundant annoyance to me. It was, from my prideful perspective, a speed bump, when all I wanted to do was speed! I thought of her as hindering me from much of what I wanted to do, not realizing that all she wanted was for me to consider her and her needs. She was constantly reaching out to me to help, and I was just as consistently pushing away her hand.

As you may be able to imagine, our relationship began to erode fast. I was unwilling to change for quite a while, and what's incredible to me is that while it seemed I would never change, she held on anyway. She had no doubt cleaved unto what was good! She was claw deep in the promises of God's Word as she purposed to show me love even when love was not reciprocated. This is the good of a godly wife – she doesn't easily let go. It's the unbreakable promises of God that keep her hoping, even sometimes against hope, and brother, I don't know about you, but that's the sort of woman I need by my side. I need a woman that isn't going to throw in the towel every time our relationship is up against the ropes and we're battling to stay on our feet. I need a woman that's going to see the best in me even when that man hasn't yet been developed. I need her to see past my light-colored mane and spoiled fruit and envision me bearing more of the fruit of the Spirit.

If you've found such a woman, you'd be a wise man to cleave unto her and never let her go. If you're still on the prowl, take what I say to heart and don't settle. This is by no means an excuse for us to be what we want and refuse to change. My wife was wise to hold on because she knew of the Spirit within me. She knew that there was a common faith in Christ between us, and that change would be inevitable for me because of the Spirit of God dwelling inside. She knew that it was only a matter of time.

She will do him good and not evil all the days of her life.

PROVERBS 31:12

Another great benefit of having a godly wife is that because she is good, she in turn treats her husband and family good. It goes back to fruit. Jesus said in Matthew 12:33, "Either make the tree good, and his fruit good; or else make the tree corrupt, and his fruit corrupt: for the tree is known by his fruit." The greatest blessing in having a godly wife is the assurance that she is in fact good; she's right with God. Her heart is changed, enabling her to desire what is good for her husband and children – those things that are good from a biblical standard of goodness. Such a woman is what I call a perpetual blessing; she's the gift that keeps on giving.

I encourage you, brother, to consider your marital relationship and give some serious thought to your wife and what she brings to your life and your children's lives. Even if your wife isn't a godly wife, you've found a good thing, nonetheless. Even if she isn't the Christian woman you desire her to be, you may have to see the woman before she is developed. Until then, cleave unto her and ride it out as you put your trust in God.

A Good Calling

So far, we've discussed the need for us to cleave unto God's Word in times of trial and our wives and relationship when the winds are blowing contrary. As I've stated before, recapturing the heart of your pride is a buffalo-sized reward, and anything worth having will require a fight to obtain it. These are two irreplaceable resources available to us that we should purpose to take full advantage of. Next, I want to examine our need to cleave unto our good calling.

What do we think of when we hear the word "calling"? Do we envision the red and green buttons that pop up on the face of our phones whenever someone's trying to call us? What exactly do we associate with this word? For me, I think of someone who is in a much higher position shouting down to another to come up higher. I define a calling as an invitation to go higher, further, and deeper with God.

Every man that God ever used to fulfill His perfect will was first called. They were invited to go beyond the limitations of their natural lives. God invited Abraham to become the father of many nations, an achievement beyond him had he declined and continued along the natural path of his life. Moses' invitation was presented to him at the burning bush. Again, we see God calling him out of his natural life into one that He had prepared for him. King David was just another shepherd before God sent him a personal invitation by the demand of the Prophet Samuel. Later, in the New Testament, we see Jesus doing the exact same thing that God has always done. We see Him inviting the common men we now know as the twelve apostles to follow Him, and this invitation was no doubt the beginning of a calling to go higher, further, and deeper than they ever anticipated with God. This is how God communicates to us initially – through the form of an invitation. What follows is always beyond our wildest imaginations.

Have you become acquainted with your calling yet? Do you know to where God is inviting you? It doesn't have to be a complicated thing to figure out. It's actually very simple. His invitation is to Himself, for where else would height, and length, and depth lead us?

And we know that all things work together for good to them that love God, to them who are the called according to his purpose. For whom he did foreknow, he also did predestinate to be conformed to the image of his Son, that he might be the firstborn among many brethren.

ROMANS 8:28-29

Brother, we're called to be conformed into the image of Christ. This means that God's purpose for our lives is that we resemble His Son more and more as each day passes. Often, we complicate what it means to be called by God. We think that it must encompass some sort of grand vision or heavenly revelation. This word "calling" either confuses or frightens us into spiritual idleness, but I want you to know that your calling is as simple as an oil change. You're called to be like Jesus in every way, and that, my friend, will keep you occupied for a lifetime.

Mind Meld

I've mentioned *Star Trek* either once or twice thus far, so you'll find no surprise in my use of another *Trek* analogy. One of the neat things I like about the original series is Gene Roddenberry's creation of the Vulcan species. Roddenberry's dream of a people renowned for their superior strength and emotionless intelligence was brought to life and best represented by the character Spock. But more impressive than his ability to throw a man clear across a room or understand the deepest mysteries the universe could present was his ability to perform the infamous mind meld.

This foreign talent consisted of him positioning his fingers in a specialized manner, making contact with various points on his subject's face and temple, and saying the now famous phrase, "My mind to your mind; my thoughts to your thoughts." Using this ability would enable him to gain entrance into the mind of another and thereby meld his mind with theirs. When melded, he could share his thoughts with his subjects. Jesus desires to do the same with us.

Let this mind be in you, which was also in Christ Jesus.

PHILIPPIANS 2:5

We are to become one with Him in mind and Spirit. The Scripture beckons us to permit the mind of Christ to be our own. It won't just happen someday when we're old and grey. We won't just suddenly have the mind of Christ. This is something that requires day-to-day acceptance. The Scripture says, "Let this mind be in you." We must willingly accept this mind as our own while purposefully shunning our old carnal mentality. If Jesus could physically touch us, maybe He'd perform a mind meld of His own: *My mind to your mind; My thoughts to your thoughts.*

His purpose for us is for us to put off the old man and put on the new man which is fashioned in mind after Him.

Lie not one to another, seeing that ye have put off the old man with his deeds; And have put on the new man, which is renewed in knowledge after the image of him that created him:

COLOSSIANS 3:9-10

Here we see that the new man is renewed in knowledge. He has the knowledge of the Scriptures down deep within him. He and Christ are melded together.

Purpose within your heart today to cleave unto what is good. The promises within God's Word, the success of your marriage, and your God-given calling are all buffalo-sized rewards that won't come easily. You will have to sink your claws into what is good and ride it out.

Make it your daily commitment to live your life by faith and not by sight. Refuse to accept that things will always be as they are. Begin to envision that buffalo coming down! Keep your faith strong in the Lord, knowing that He is with you. Adopt the kind of faith that cleaves to what is good even when it seems that all is bad.

Eight

The Mane Attraction

Husbands, love your wives, even as Christ also loved the Church, and gave himself for it.

EPHESIANS 5:25

IN 2017, AARON LUKASZEWSKI, A PSYCHOLOGIST AT CALIfornia State University at Fullerton, performed a study to measure a woman's level of attractiveness toward men with varying body types. Of the 160 college-aged women that were surveyed, zero showed a statistical interest in weaker men.[23] Go figure!

Lukaszewski and his coauthors created a photo database of shirtless or tank top-wearing male college students, all from the University of California at Santa Barbara. The women were asked to judge how attractive they thought the men were on a scale of one to seven based on their body types alone. Their faces were blurred. Men were also asked how strong they thought the shirtless or semi-shirtless men were. It turned out that the men who the women thought of as most attractive were also perceived by other men as the strongest. "Perceptions of strength closely aligned with the men's actual strength," said Ben Guarino, the writer of the article published by the Washington Post.[24] Turns out, we're pretty good at comparing apples to apples. He continued, "The researchers also discovered a direct relationship between a man's rated strength and his attractiveness."[25] According to Lukaszewski, "What really explains the lion's share in attractiveness is how strong a man looks."[26]

The researchers identified a strong body as a signal that communicates a message to both spectating males and females. An individual that appears to be physically toned and in shape usually means that they possess a strong immune system, capable of allocating more calories toward building muscle as opposed to fighting off germs. Strength was also an "indicator of one's ability to provide material and social benefits," Lukaszewski said.[27] Remember, women think long when considering a possible mate while men tend to think short. The synopsis was clear to the team of researchers, "A strong man has value as a potential protector of women and children and is desired by other men as an ally."[28]

The Value of Strength

Strength is a quality sought after by everyone in every field of work and facet of society. It's something we look for in our engines and a key feature in the protective cases for our phones and tablets. Strength is the quality we look for in our trash bags, cleaning solutions, and coffee. We require even our laundry detergent to be strong enough to freshen our less than fresh undergarments. As a people, we value strength.

Weakness, on the other hand, is just as off-putting as it sounds. We have no interest in things that are weak because they require us to work harder and more frequently than we desire. Weakness costs us our hard-earned money and strips us of our invaluable time. Weakness doesn't add to our lives but rather it takes away.

I always say life in the Army is hard on a weak soldier. The demands of Army life are just too heavy and too burdensome on his weak body and mind. The rucksack pains his back and shoulders around mile three, and he complains the remaining nine. The strong soldier, on the other hand, is fit to bear it the extent of the march without a word of grievance. The weak soldier complains because of the rigors of physical training, while the strong soldier excels and even encourages his fellow troops. Combat is no place for a weak soldier. He shudders at the sound of artillery and gunfire, while strong soldiers keep their wit. Weak soldiers tend to fizzle early on in their career. They get passed up for promotion while strong soldiers climb the ranks and end their careers at the height of their profession. Strength and leadership are like magnets with opposing poles; they attract to one another. The same could be said in the inverse about weakness. We don't want weak leadership so it should be no surprise when I say women don't want a weak man.

Take buying a home for instance. When choosing our homes, we ensure we ask the right questions: How will a home with this sort of foundation hold up against a flood? Does it stand on a concrete or crawlspace foundation? Is the roof equipped to handle heavy weathering over an extended period of time? How old are the pipes? Is the heating and cooling system outdated? Will this home in this particular neighborhood appreciate in value over time? The list can continue as far as your interest and proper concern will take you.

What about hiring a potential employee? Strength is certainly one value employers look for in their would-be workers. They'll ask questions to get a feel for their ability to carry out the responsibilities of the job: Do you have any experience in this field? What are some of your strengths? What are some of your weaknesses? Why should we hire you over our other applicants? How long do you intend to work for our company? These are just a few questions you might be asked by an employer interested in gaining the full picture of a potential investment, and that's just what it is – an investment. Whether we're buying a home, hiring a potential employee, or sitting across from a person of interest over dinner, we're in the beginning stages of making a long-term investment.

Like employers and potential home buyers, women ask the hard questions early so that they don't have to pay for it later. They look for strength in men like you and I because of the great value strength adds to their lives. It's a simple formula: the stronger you are the more attractive you are in the sight of your potential wife. Remember, according to Lukaszewski's study, strength is an indicator of your ability to provide material and social benefits. She needs to know that the roof won't leak when the rains descend much longer than anticipated. She needs to know that when the floods of indifference, financial hardship, poor health, and spiritual trial begin to rise, your house will still stand through it all. The best way to assure her of this is to show yourself strong and commit to developing a full black mane.

Lukaszewski may have determined a man's attractiveness to be based on his physical appearance, but we know that the true strength of a man is hidden within. Good looks may strike her interest, but it's the stuff on the inside that'll win her heart. It's the fruit of a man's spirit that broadcasts his level of strength, just as the mane tells on a male lion. Your potential wife is looking for an asset to add to her life, not a liability that will only cause her heartache and pain in the future.

The Mark of Protection

In December of 2020, I surveyed a group of women in the interest of learning what women find most attractive about their potential husbands. I wanted to know what was the number one quality in a man that women look for. I presented each woman with a list of eight qualities and instructed them to select their top three and provide a brief explanation as to why they chose each quality. Here's the list of qualities they had to choose from:

1. Physical appeal
2. Protective ability (emotional, spiritual, physical)
3. Leadership ability
4. Financial stability
5. Demonstrated character
6. Masculinity
7. Presence
8. Drive

Of the eight qualities listed above, 83 percent of the women surveyed selected *protective ability* as the number one quality they look for in a potential husband. Remember, statistically, women are unattracted to weaker men. They need to know that the man they choose is capable of defending them and their children physically, emotionally, and spiritually. As Lukaszewski uncovered in his study, it's strength that draws the attention of a woman from a physical standpoint. She prefers a man that appears well put together, one who is fit and capable. As I disclosed in the very first chapter of this book, lionesses are no different.

The mane of a male lion is the mark of protection. It's the one thing a lioness will closely observe to determine the strength and capability of a male lion. It tells her a story that she needs to hear if she's to commit to him; his mane reveals his quality. To refresh your memory, allow me to briefly recall the insightful field study that substantiated this fact.

Remember the study that involved life-sized lion dummies with manes varying in color in chapter one? It was the dark maned male that won the attention and mating rights of each lioness as they approached, while the blond maned male wasn't given as much as the time of day.

Whether you're a married or single man reading this chapter, I'll have you know that the woman of your interest, whether your wife or potential wife, desires protection. It's how she's designed. A woman needs to know that she's secure with you before she either commits to marriage or feels confident in the already established relationship.

Likewise, ye husbands, dwell with them according to knowledge, giving honour unto the wife, as unto the weaker vessel, and as being heirs together of the grace of life; that your prayers be not hindered.

1 PETER 3:7

As husbands and future husbands, God expects us to handle our wives with tenderness and sensitivity. I know that I only speak for myself when I say it can be incredibly easy to be insensitive with my wife with how I communicate and interact with her. I couldn't tell you how many times my wife has softly expressed her preference to a gentle rub on the arms as opposed to poking and tickling her out of play. Sure, there's times when that is okay, but it goes back to what Peter said, "Dwell with them according to knowledge." There's a time and a place for such antics, but the time is not all the time. For her, a gentle rub is a reassurance of my love for her, and it communicates to her that I'm listening, I see her, and that I'm mindful of her. It's an act of love, which is precisely the mark of protection.

In Galatians 5, love is the first quality identified as a contributing element of the fruit of the Spirit of God. If the fruit of the Spirit were an apple, love would be the stem. It's the element from which all other qualities branch out from. But how does love relate to our manes, and how does it have anything to do with attractiveness? I'm glad you asked! Remember, even as the mane is indicative of a lion's state of health, so the fruit of a man's spirit is an honest snapshot of his spiritual fitness. So, the condition of our love plays a significant part in the coloration of our manes, which in turn either attracts or detracts the woman of your interest.

We reveal what sort of men we are simply by our day-to-day life. Our lives speak more about us than our words, and it doesn't take long for a woman to gain the full picture of a man. If she gives you her number, that means your first impression caught her interest and she'd like to assess further. At this stage, I wouldn't celebrate just yet. This is a mere invitation for further evaluation. If you find yourself seated, casually sharing a meal with her, know that you're still under scrutiny. Everything you say and don't say is communicating to her what sort of man you are. The little subtilties expressed through your words, body language, and character are all telling her a story; they're revealing your quality.

As lionesses look to the mane for an honest assessment of their would-be mates, so women search for fruit within their potential husbands. She may not even realize that's what she's doing, but it is. She's looking for quality. She's on the lookout for qualities that prove your ability to protect her and your future family. Questions like, does he listen well or does he genuinely care for what I'm communicating, play within her mind. Is he thoughtful and considerate of others? Does he put others before himself? Is he selfish and self-centered? Does he only think of himself and his own interests? These and so many more questions will a women sift through in her mind before making her decision to marry, because marriage is a long-term commitment.

Of the many qualities a woman looks for in a man, his ability to protect her tops the list. I think we as men, for the most part, know what it means to protect a woman physically. Maybe we imagine jumping in front of a car for her, physically fighting for her, or defending her in some fashion. There are times when I'm out with my wife when I'm thinking of possible scenarios where I might have to protect her. I don't know if you've ever done this, but I do it all the time. These scenarios can be a bit extreme, but they always involve me defending her.

On Monday, I'm fighting off three knife-wielding robbers at the market. Later in the week, I'm carrying her and my three children on my shoulders down a fire escape, evading a burning building. At two o'clock in the morning every other night, I'm popping out of bed at the sound of the faintest screech to wrestle with some burglar as I direct my wife to get the kids and lock the bedroom door. I refuse to believe I'm the only guy that thinks of these things, but if I am, then so be it. I know it's only the testosterone playing with my head, keeping me ready for whatever.

Simply put, man is wired to protect and defend woman. That's just how God made us. Just as women are designed to be protected, we are designed to protect. When this is the understanding of both the man and woman, it helps to bring the relationship into harmony because the roles aren't blurred or misunderstood.

But what does it mean to protect a woman emotionally and spiritually? If women desire to be protected, how do we protect what we cannot see? Her emotions and spirituality are intangible elements of her that are as real as the ink on this page. So, how do you protect her from what is invisible? The answer is found in scripture.

Husbands, love your wives, even as Christ also loved the Church, and gave himself for it.

EPHESIANS 5:25

God simply tells us to love her as Christ loved us. If you're reading this and you're married, God is telling you the key to unlocking your wife's complete confidence and trust is for you to love her unconditionally. If you're single and you desire to marry someday, I encourage you to become acquainted with the love of Jesus Christ, and to allow His love to become your own. Isn't it the love of God that protects us? Isn't it the love of God that makes it possible for us to overcome eternal destruction (John 3:16)?

It was the blood of Christ, an act of sacrificial love, that made it possible for us to be justified in the sight of God, thus protecting us from His eternal wrath. It was His love that protected us and eventually attracted us to Him. We found great value in coming to a Savior that demonstrated such great love toward us. In like manner, it'll be your demonstrated love that attracts the woman in your life or to your life. But if the number one quality women look for in their potential husbands is the ability to protect, and love is the mark of protection, how do we demonstrate this quality of love? Well, before we can live in love, we must first learn what love is.

Charity suffereth long, and is kind; charity envieth not; charity vaunt not itself, is not puffed up, Doth not behave itself unseemly, seeketh not her own, is not easily provoked, thinketh no evil, rejoiceth not in iniquity, but rejoiceth in the truth. Beareth all things, believeth all things, hopeth all things, endureth all things.

1 CORINTHIANS 13:4-7

This is an incredibly insightful description of what love actually is. Love is so often poorly represented by the world. The world tells us that if we buy her gifts, she'll know that we love her, when the real gift we ought to be giving her is the gift of a kind spirit or a humble and tender-hearted disposition. Sure, gifts are a great way of expressing our love for our wives but not when the former is left undone. If we maintain unkind attitudes toward our wives and we don't put them before ourselves in everything, then our gifts amount to little to nothing. What good is a surprise trip to a foreign country when your company is sour? That only makes for a long miserable trip. To give you a visual of what the quality of love looks like, I've listed each adjective that describes love below:

Love is	**Love is not**
Patient	Impatient
Kind	Unkind
Content with its own possessions	Envious
Speaks well of others	Boastful
Humble	Proud
Careful to behave appropriately	Inappropriately behaved
A seeker of good things for others	A self-seeking quality
Self-tamed	Uncontrolled
Pure of mind	Evil minded
Joyful in righteousness and truth	Joyful in sin and unrighteousness
Strong	Weak
Faithful	Faithless
Hopeful	Hopeless
Able to bear everything	Broken under pressure
Victorious	Failure

These are the elements or character traits that will ultimately reveal to a woman whether you're capable of loving and protecting her. These characteristics are low hanging fruit in the eyes of any sensible woman; they're the mark of protection distinguishing you as a man of noble character and spirit. Endeavor to strengthen each of these elements in your life, and it won't be long before your mane catches the eye of your future Sarabi.

Nine

Apples to Apples

Be not deceived: evil communications corrupt good manners.

– 1 CORINTHIANS 15:33

CHOICES. AREN'T THEY THE POWER OF MAN? YOU KNOW, like Superman can break through impenetrable barriers and lift buildings and the Flash has supersonic speed, we have the power to choose. But we don't think of our God-given power of choice as a power. In fact, we think nothing of it at all.

When we choose to spend our days binge-watching our favorite television series when we could be doing something a bit more productive, we think nothing of it. We don't stop to consider this power when we choose to bombard our bellies with a barrage of bite-sized brownies, chocolates, and other sugary delights, when we could just as conveniently reach for a healthier option. With every swipe of our overly-used credit cards, we think nothing of the ten dollars here, seven dollars there, and twenty-nine ninety-nine elsewhere. We simply swipe and think nothing of it. We undermine the power that exists in every one of our life's choices.

Choices are of no significance to the man who chooses to live his life without purpose and intent; he just goes with the flow. The problem with this is that the flow almost always leads to a great and terrible drop-off! Anyone with a nonchalant attitude toward the decisions they make each and every day is heading in the wrong direction...and fast.

You see, binge-watching your favorite show may be okay for one or two nights. The problem comes into play when we find that our periodic spurts of entertainment fixes have matured into a full-blown habit and worse – it's getting in the way of productivity. We don't see our decision to snack on sweets here and there as a big deal until a doctor informs us that our blood sugar is abnormally high or the scale becomes our enemy. The small purchases that we make aren't a bother or cause for alarm until we see that our insignificant swipes have snowballed into a massive debt!

It's during these moments of effect that we begin to realize just how powerful our choices can be. It's when we begin to feel the brunt of our choices that we realize how poorly we've used our power. Without a doubt, our very lives are constructed of the choices we make every day. We're the summation of every one of our decisions so it's critical we gain a good understanding of this power God has given us. It's of absolute necessity that we tap into this power of choice that lies dormant in the lives of so many men. We don't want to be men who just go with the flow. Men who live carelessly and without purpose call misery home and make defeat their close companion. They care not to become any better than they already are. They're okay with living less than they were intended.

But not us! Mane-bearers don't settle for less! Dark-maned men cringe at the thought of squandering their life's potential. We desire to be men of respectable character and extraordinary faith. We want to be men who live life on purpose, fit to represent our Lord well. We want to be men who influence everyone we encounter to turn from their wretched lives of sin and shame and pursue after a wonderful Savior. But in order for us to become such men, we must realize the power that our Heavenly Father has given us. If we're to influence men for the Kingdom of God's sake, we will have to consider our choices.

If Life Were a Canvas

In 1983, a popular television show aired on PBS with a man by the name of Robert Norman Ross or Bob Ross as it's host. *The Joy of Painting* presented Bob as a friendly artist who made painting beautiful landscapes so simple anyone with the proper materials could do it. He'd invite the viewers to join him as he began to paint his new piece, casually giving them step by step instructions along the way. With each stroke of the brush, viewers were able to turn blank canvases into creatively crafted landscapes by the end of Bob's episode. All the viewers had to do was follow Bob's instructions and eventually each individual stroke of the brush would climax into a visually appealing piece of artwork.

Now imagine if each choice we made moment by moment were the stroke of a paint brush and life was a canvas. Would our paintings be works of visual art or a catastrophe? Right now, in this very moment, how would your life's painting look? Would our life-paintings be to the glory of God or to our shame and regret? We must be mindful that, like painting a work of art, the individual choices we make every day will eventually culminate. With every decision, we're taking strokes upon our life's canvas effectively presenting our lives to the world as fruitful or not. Our choices directly affect our testimony for Christ, so it's imperative we give heed to the decisions we make.

Ponder the path of thy feet, and let all thy ways be established.

PROVERBS 4:26

I often reference the verse above in my writings because I like the visual image I get from the simplicity of the instructions. Solomon is writing to his children in this verse as in many other verses throughout the book of Proverbs. He's speaking from the perspective of a loving and caring father who wishes to teach his children in the way of wisdom. He says, "Ponder the path of thy feet." In other words, he says, "Think intently about where you're going." Too often we don't give enough attention to thought before we begin something or commit to someone. We're not careful to consider both the way and the individuals we're choosing to journey with before we take the first step.

We see this proven through the ever-steady divorce rate in our country as more and more couples fail to stand the test of time. A total of about 750,000 marriages threw in the towel in 2019.[29] We see it validated by the staggering number of children recorded as living in foster care in year 2020 — a total of 424,000 to be exact.[30] Learning of these realities causes me to think of how many marriages could have overcome the challenges of marital life and how many little ones could've avoided the hardships of growing up in an unfamiliar and often times unsafe foster care environment, if only we would take the time to think before we act.

Too often, we're thinking with the wrong head, which often leads to children born out of wedlock having to face the jungle of life without a present father. Our children need fathers who will actively patrol the territory of their lives, not only be the guy who buys them nice things on their birthdays and on holidays. They need guardians, and men that will take the time to discover and excavate their hidden potential. They need lion-like examples of fathers who believe it's their inherited responsibility to care for and protect their own.

It's overwhelmingly clear that we're not taking the time to analyze the path before we decide to move forward. We're getting blindsided by pregnancy notices and finding that we're ill prepared to take care of ourselves, let alone another person. I can't tell you how many men I know and have known that fall into this category. Men who parent their children from afar, which is actually an oxymoron. Parenting cannot be done from afar, it must be up close and personal if we're to have any godly influence over our children. Men who believe that they're upholding their responsibilities as fathers from afar haven't understood what it means to be a father and what it means to be a parent. But it doesn't have to be this way. All it takes is the discipline to slow down, think, and consider the outcome of our decisions.

What Solomon says next can only be accomplished when we've followed the first instructions. He says, "And let all thy ways be established," or in layman's terms, "After you've considered with great thought where you intend to go, go in the way of wisdom." If we neglect to take the time to ponder on where we intend to go in life, we will have made a terribly dangerous mistake. When we refuse to consider our direction in life, we willfully walk upon unstable and unestablished ground. When we're not intentional about our choices, it's as if we're painting blindly. The result is that we make a mess of our canvases.

The Bad Apple Effect

Of the many choices we must make as men, one of the more important ones is who we choose to identify with. The men we choose to befriend directly influence our lives, either for better or worse. We're either helped or hindered by our fellowship.

There's a law of impressions that exists within our world that causes us to take on the likeness of those with whom we are closely familiar. Familiarity ranges beyond just physical relationships with friends, colleagues, and family members. This law of impressions comes into play with everything, and everyone we interact with. The television series we follow to the books we read, the websites we visit, the videos we stream, and the newsfeeds we scroll through are all leaving an impression upon our lives. We must, as I've mentioned before, purpose to guide what we see and hear and who we spend our time with because these associations have a way of impressing themselves onto us.

The Word of God has a reoccurring theme throughout its entirety of the importance of maintaining proper associations. Israel was warned of God not to become as their heathen neighbors who worshipped other gods. Jesus cautioned His disciples to beware of the doctrine of the pharisees, and the Apostle Paul instructs all believers not to be unequally yoked together with unbelievers. God's position on how His children ought to choose their friends remains constant through and through. Paul made it abundantly clear when he said, "What communion hath light with darkness?" (2 Corinthians 6:14). This theme didn't occur in Scripture by happenstance. God is trying to tell us something very important. He's trying to open our eyes to the reality of impressions and how easily they can cause us to stray from Him.

If you've ever purchased a bag of apples, maybe you've noticed something many of us tend not to consider. The bag containing the apples always has holes throughout it, and there's a good reason for it. You see, apples give off a gaseous substance called ethylene during their ripening process. As this gas pulsates off the apple, it causes neighboring fruits to ripen at an accelerated rate. A bad apple in a sealed bag full of good apples will spoil the whole bag. Ethylene is where we get the common phrase, "One bad apple can spoil the barrel," and this is also true for all mediums of influence just as much as it is for apples.

Be not deceived: evil communications corrupt good manners.

1 CORINTHIANS 15:33

As we purpose to walk in the way of fruitfulness, God will certainly put His finger on our choice of friends. Another translation of this scripture says, "Bad company corrupts good character." It's impossible to develop a dark mane while insisting on keeping the company of men who care not to develop the fruit of the Spirit in their lives. When we find that the men we associate ourselves with have no desire to grow spiritually, it's a sure sign that we must move on. If we continue to walk with them while trying to live for the Lord, we will eventually stray from the will of God. It's impossible to walk in two opposite directions at the same time. We either go north or we go south; we either go east or we go west, but we will never be able to go north-south or east-west.

Men who have already decided in their hearts that they're not going to follow the Lord and live according to His desires are bad apples. They will only grow worse as time passes. We must first rid our lives of the bad apples in our company before we begin the process of developing our manes. It's a decision that isn't always easy, but it's one that is vitally necessary. This may mean that you walk alone for some time, and if that's the case, don't fret. Trust the Lord in your time of solitude, and He will guide you – I know from experience.

I distinctively remember when I realized I couldn't hang with the guys I used to hang with. It's as if I came to myself in the sense that my eyes were now open to the detriment maintaining such friendships would have caused to my future and spiritual development. I realized for the first time in my life that my friends were no good for my future, and that was a hard notion to accept. They were guys I loved and cared about deeply, guys I felt a sense of loyalty to. But in my time of seeking the Lord as a young man, He made it abundantly clear to me that I had to sever ties. He put His finger on my friends. His plans for my life involved me moving in a direction they weren't going.

It was during the summer before my senior year in high school when I came face to face with the reality of the decision I had to make. I distinctively remember in a moment of solitude weeping as I came to terms with the fact that I couldn't continue in life with them as my close friends. It hurt me to know I had to move on without them, but I was more willing to endure the pain of letting go than to suffer the consequences of holding on. It was my soul's salvation at stake. It was my development as a man and my growth as a mane-bearer at risk. Up until that moment of realization, I was of no use to God. I was a stiff piece of clay on the Lord's pottery wheel. I made it hard for His hands to mold, to shape, and to create. But when I chose to let go and move forward, it's as if the material of my life had softened, making it easier for God to mold me into the man He wanted me to be.

There comes a time in every man's life when we must choose between our future and our friends. It's a time inherent in manhood where we must quit playing games and decide what's best for us and the calling God has on our lives. Our decision to maintain friendships that are not progressive will eventually bring about a bad apple effect in our lives. We'll find ourselves wondering why we haven't become more refined in our service to God, why we haven't borne more fruit, or why it seems we've only grown worse with time when we choose to keep the bad apples close. I don't know about you, but God's plans for me are too precious for me to allow anyone to get in the way of them. I dare not squander my life's potential on a few familiar faces.

A Mane to Be Matched

In the world of psychology, there's what's known as the Social Comparison Theory, which describes the natural drive people have to compare themselves to others. It's a theory built upon the idea that we evaluate our opinions, abilities, and character traits against that of others.[31]

For instance, as a teen, I boxed for a short span of time. During my first few weeks of training, I began to naturally compare myself to the guys I would spar with. If it was clear to me that a guy was better than I was, I wanted to emulate his hand speed, foot movement, or technique. My desire to improve as a boxer enabled me to see his advancement as an opportunity for my own. On the other hand, if I perceived the next guy to be a cut below me, I would feel some sense of accomplishment simply because I was better than the other guy. These two examples are referred to as upward and downward social comparison and it means just as it sounds.

It can be comforting when we choose to accompany ourselves with men we perceive to be a cut below us. Maybe their education isn't as high or their profession not as respectable. Maybe their lack of character is something we secretly find advantageous, something to be capitalized on. This sort of approach to friendship may seem odd, but this is how a lot of men choose their friends. You see, when you're not serious about being a man and accepting all the responsibilities that are inherent in being a man, you'll settle for merely appearing to be one. It'll make you feel good when you're surrounded by other men who are worse off than you because in comparison to them, you're *the* man! When you measure yourself against them, your achievements and material gain always outweighs theirs. It strokes your ego to see that you're doing better than they are, and from this, you draw your own opinion of your personal quality and value. But that's a distorted viewpoint of self, and I'd even venture to say delusional! The mouse is only giant to the ant, and just as the ant is a terrible reference of measure for the mouse, so fruitless men are rotten indicators of our own level of fruitfulness.

We're not good because we compare ourselves to men who are worse off than us in terms of fruitfulness. Yet many men walk around thinking themselves right with God because they're not living nearly as bad as a few guys they know. They think, "In comparison to such and such, I'm doing good." If our standard of righteousness is founded upon the failures of others, then our unit of measure isn't true to scale. We're comparing ourselves to the wrong people, in fact, we shouldn't be comparing ourselves to people at all. We're gathering our identity from a downward social comparison when we should be finding our truest measure by comparing ourselves upward to Christ.

As for me, I will behold thy face in righteousness: I shall be satisfied when I awake, with thy likeness.

PSALM 17:15

Jesus is the only man we should be looking to as an example of what right looks like in terms of fruitfulness. Of course, God gives us men after his heart and likeness that we can follow, but it's Christ we should desire to emulate ultimately. The reason for this is because Jesus is the perfect example of a man that embodies every element of the fruit of the Spirit. The Bible tells us that God didn't give Him the Spirit by measure (John 3:34). This means that the Spirit of God had full rule and reign within His mortal body while He walked upon the earth fulfilling the will of God. It wasn't a matter of debate or a point of struggle for Jesus to submit to the will of God. He humbled Himself from the beginning as mentioned in Philippians 2:8, "And being found in fashion as a man, he humbled himself, and became obedient unto death, even the death of the cross." In His humility, the Spirit of God found a worthy vessel and space meet to begin His work.

Some may wonder how Jesus was capable of honoring and pleasing God in all things. How can a man deny His flesh all the time and every time? It's not trigonometry. The man allowed the Spirit of God to rule in His heart, and His victory over the workings of the flesh is ours if we follow His example.

And that's just what this chapter is about – forsaking the examples of the world and following the example of Christ. It's about ridding our lives of people we know within our hearts are no good for us. It's about ceasing to compare ourselves against ourselves and beginning to measure our lives against the life of Christ. It's time we make Him our closest friend and companion. It's time we quit neglecting reading His Word for lesser interests and really purpose to get to know this God we say we know. It's time to see ourselves in pure light and trust God to give us the courage to change.

When we compare our fruit to the fruit of man, we find no need for growth. But when we compare our apples to the apples of Christ, we are made aware of our truest spiritual state. He reveals our truest quality. He's the one that makes our fruitlessness very clear. He's the one that reveals in us the poor condition of our manes. It's when we compare our apples to His that we find our truest measure and condition and are inspired to become as He is.

Back in 2012, I was an army recruit, completing my Advanced Individual Training (AIT) at Gulfport Mississippi, a Naval station located along the coast of the Gulf of Mexico. I was training to become an engineer, and as is customary in army life, my company would go for runs about three days a week. Before we'd start out on our run, we'd split into three different groups: A group, B group, and C group. C group was for the soldiers in the company that were struggling to pass their two-mile test and needed improvement. It was for the slowpokes. B group was designated for the average runners who could pass their two-mile test in under 16 minutes. Only the elite runners would dare to fall into formation with A group or "A Train" as we referred to ourselves. It was home to guys that could run two miles in eleven minutes. Even the fastest guy was challenged to keep up on some mornings. You knew that if you were running with "A Train," you were in for a hard run, and it was going to be uncomfortable the entire time. Some guys who belonged to A group would sometimes cowardly join B group out of fear. They didn't want to have to endure the discomfort of a long hard run for 45 minutes to an hour.

I happened to run with A group, and it wasn't long before I noticed another soldier in my group who made it a point to beat me in every run. I wish I could remember his name, but I don't. For the sake of this illustration, we'll just call him Julio. Julio had it out for me. Every morning that we formed up to run Julio would always make some sort of comment about how he was going to catch me this time. But day after day, run after run, Julio always came up short. I could always here him behind me running his hardest trying his best to catch me, even shouting at times, "I'm going to catch you Hobson!" But he just couldn't.

As time went on, I could see that Julio was becoming frustrated with his inability to pass me. His frustration developed into somewhat of an obsession, to where passing me was all he would think about while out on the run. It didn't matter whether he came in first. All he cared for was passing Hobson. Until one day, after exhaustedly finishing a run, Julio, in a moment of humility asked me, "Why is it so hard to catch you?"

He wanted to know the underlining secret that I used as motivation to never slow down, and I told him, "I don't race against you guys. It's the time that matters to me. Time is my competitor."

You see, I was an elite runner not because I was trying to keep up with the other men in my group – had I done that the roles might've been reversed and I might've been the one chasing Julio! It was the methodical clicking of the numbers on my wristwatch that enabled me to excel. I had a time in mind while Julio had me in mind.

I imagine that an Olympic runner doesn't assess his performance by looking to the guy running next to him. If the gold medal is to be achieved, it'll be because he had a time and a goal in mind before he ever stepped foot on the track. His standard is higher than man, which is precisely the reason men will stand in awe when he becomes the new record holder. If Olympians measured themselves against themselves, records would scarcely be broken. It's when a man with a wild eye decides to look beyond mere mortals that he achieves the impossible.

If thou hast run with the footmen, and they have wearied thee, then how canst thou contend with horses? and if in the land of peace, wherein thou trustedst, they wearied thee, then how wilt thou do in the swelling of Jordan?

JEREMIAH 12:5

When it comes to developing as men of God, we must hold ourselves to a standard that is higher than man. We too must, with wild eyes, dare to go beyond the status quo and look further than the silhouettes of men. Jesus, my friend, is the standard every man needs. He's our figurative wristwatch; He's the One we check with continuously to ensure we're hitting our marks and on track to glory!

Wherefore seeing we also are compassed about with so great a cloud of witnesses, let us lay aside every weight, and the sin which doth so easily beset us, and let us run with patience the race that is set before us, Looking unto Jesus the author and finisher of our faith; who for the joy that was set before him endured the cross, despising the shame, and is set down at the right hand of the throne of God.

HEBREWS 12:1-2

We sometimes aim too low in life. We make a habit out of assessing whether we're doing well by looking to the people around us when we should be looking to Jesus. Our salvation begins and ends with Him so it's Him that we should look to as our example from start to finish. We should seek all our instructions for living a life pleasing to God from Him. He knows how to please God better than any man as He Himself says in John 8:29, "And he that sent me is with me: the Father hath not left me alone; for I do always those things that please him." Jesus is the only man that can truthfully say that He always pleases the Father in all things. His life is our blueprint for living victoriously. His fruit is what we all should desire to emulate.

If He were a lion, His mane would be midnight black without any variation of color. In terms of testosterone, He's our conquering King. He possesses what I refer to as spiritual aggression, which means He never passively allows Satan to have his way. He, on His own accord, went into the enemy's territory by choosing to be born of flesh, robbed Satan of his power over man through His victory over sin and death, and made a way for all to experience the privilege of knowing Him. If that's not lion-like behavior, I don't know what is!

While Satan by his territorial nature walks about seeking whom to devour, Jesus by His love seeks to save all who are lost. There are two lions roving about the earth: one seeks to devour the other seeks to develop. When Jesus gets ahold of our hearts there's not a devil in hell or a man on earth that can remove us from His will. He says in John 10:28, "And I give unto them eternal life; and they shall never perish, neither shall any man pluck them out of my hand." This is our King. This is our example of bearing our manes properly. So, in terms of spiritual testosterone, none can compare. In terms of fruit, well, the Scriptures speak for themselves:

The Love of Christ

But God commendeth his love toward us, in that, while we were yet sinners, Christ died for us.

Romans 5:8

The Joy of Christ

Looking unto Jesus the author and finisher of our faith; who for the joy that was set before him endured the cross, despising the shame, and is set down at the right hand of the throne of God.

Hebrews 12:2

The Peace of Christ

For unto us a child is born, unto us a son is given: and the government shall be upon his shoulder: and his name shall be called Wonderful, Counsellor, The mighty God, The everlasting Father, The Prince of Peace.

Isaiah 9:6

The Patience of Christ

He was oppressed, and he was afflicted, yet he opened not his mouth: he is brought as a lamb to the slaughter, and as a sheep before her shearers is dumb, so he openeth not his mouth.

Isaiah 53:7

The Gentleness of Christ

And they brought young children to him, that he should touch them: and his disciples rebuked those that brought them. But when Jesus saw it, he was much displeased, and said unto them, Suffer the little children to come unto me, and forbid them not: for of such is the kingdom of God. Verily I say unto you, Whosoever shall not receive the kingdom of God as a little child, he shall not enter therein. And he took them up in his arms, put his hands upon them, and blessed them.

Mark 10:13-16

The Goodness of Christ

And Jesus said, Somebody hath touched me: for I perceive that virtue is gone out of me.

Luke 8:46

The Faith of Christ

And, behold, there arose a great tempest in the sea, insomuch
that the ship was covered with the waves: but he was asleep.

Matthew 8:24

The Meekness (Submissiveness) of Christ

Who, when he was reviled, reviled not again; when he suffered, he threatened not; but committed himself to him that
judgeth righteously.

1 Peter 2:23

The Control of Christ

Thinkest thou that I cannot now pray to my Father, and he
shall presently give me more than twelve legions of angels?
But how then shall the scriptures be fulfilled, that thus
it must be?

Matthew 26:53-54

I've only chosen one example of our Lord's embodiment of
each element of the fruit of the Spirit, but there are several
for each element. It's clear that the Lion of Judah's mane is
that of completeness and totality. His quality is unmatched,
which is why His mane is what we should purpose to match.

Purpose to make Jesus your closest friend by taking the
time each day to pray and learn of His ways through reading,
studying, and meditating upon Scripture. It'll only be a matter of time before He begins to impress Himself upon you,
and you'll notice yourself growing more and more each day.
When you've chosen to make the Lion of Judah your closest
companion, your mane will inevitably darken as a result of
learning and adopting His ways.

Ten

The Appeal of Passion

Thou shalt love the Lord thy God with all thy heart, and with all thy soul, and with all thy mind.

– MATTHEW 22:37

I HAD A CONVERSATION WITH MY FATHER NOT LONG AGO over a video call when he made mention of the Vikings. He had been watching a series that focused upon their way of life. I could tell that this television series was of great interest to him. It was clear to me that he was very much intrigued in the way these Vikings were portrayed: rough, rugged savages who lived by their own moral code. He found their fierce loyalty to one another and their passion for their way of life appealing. He was completely captivated by their principles, how they lived without apology, why they were who they were, and that they weren't ashamed of it.

It didn't matter that they were notorious for dropping anchor and storming savagely through European coastal villages, leaving whole regions in ruin. The fact that these Vikings were known for destroying homes and tearing apart families wasn't a cause for concern in my father's mind. It was the passion for their way of life as depicted in the television series that he found appealing. Their record of recklessly and unapologetically devastating European monasteries was, along with all the other devastation they caused, overshadowed by their depicted loyalty and heart-binding duty to their pagan way of life.

This is the power of passion even if it's perceived and felt only through the medium of a television screen. Passion will cause us to ignore the facts because it's mesmerizing to witness a human life so devoted and so completely enthralled with a certain philosophy or belief that they'd go to any length to live it out. Their impenitent attitude is the fragrance that lures the aimless soul. Passion has a very strong appeal. We feel it in our hearts when we're sitting on our living room couches watching our favorite team compete in the playoffs. We see it in the lives of people inordinately loyal to a particular political party or public figure. We witness passion within the lives of so called "workaholics" who have a hard time knowing when to put the hammer down. The sight of passion in others reaches down and touches the center of our deepest aspirations, causing our heartrates to rise and our thoughts to surge. We see passion and we want it; we want to be passionate ourselves.

We've all seen the response of fiery boxing fans when their champ is on the ropes. We've witnessed the man in the crowd fold his fists tightly, frown intensely, and throw some jabs of his own as he shouts his champ to victory. We may not know exactly what to be passionate about, but we know we want to be passionate about something. We want to know what it feels like to be so dedicated to something that we'd be willing to go 12 rounds with our worst enemy. We want to fight for something. We want to find something worth dying for. We want to experience the passion we see in others.

But for many of us, we're not passionate about anything. We live day in and day out with hearts lukewarm. Our eyes carry bags strong enough to bear the burden of unrealized aspirations. We're tired of exhausting energy in a field or way of life we're not passionate about.

So, it's no wonder we feel intensely loyal to our favorite television series or sports team. It makes sense why we would flock to the coliseums, theatres, and stadiums. As a society, we figure if we're unsuccessful in finding our own fire, if we're not willing to find our own passion in life, then we'll just observe others as they live out theirs. We can understand why so many young people walk about with headphones in their ears listening to their favorite artist nonstop around the clock. They hear what they perceive to be someone passionate about something, and though that something may amount to nothing at all, it's appealing, nonetheless. They believe in the image that the musicians and vocal artists portray in the media.

But the thing about passion is that while others may appear to be passionate about several different pursuits, it can be misplaced and therefore channeled in the wrong direction. The Viking era is a good example of misguided passion.

There was a soldier in my unit when I was stationed in South Korea that always had a very negative attitude. He was a very off-putting sort of person who didn't have a filter, and everything he'd say was always on some level adverse and could very easily be offensive to many people. Well, when it came time for him to go on to his next assignment, I saw him smoking a cigarette in our container yard by himself. I altered my route back to the office and turned to talk with him to see how he was doing and share the gospel with him. As I ministered to him about the gospel of Christ, he mentioned that he already held to a religion and that he believed in the ideology of the Vikings. As he began to explain the fundamental principles of his religion, if that's what we're calling it, I told him, "Sounds like something someone just thought up in their head."

You see, the Vikings held to a belief that death in battle was the most honorable of deaths and that paradise or, as they called it, Valhalla awaited such bravery. They were a people who lived as heathens with no ruler to guide them. Their era lasted only about three hundred years from about A.D. 800 to 1100.[32] A key fact is that they were not Christian during a time when Christianity was spreading throughout Europe. They had no respect for Christians or religious institutions but rather took advantage of them. They were no heroes like my fellow comrade might have thought. Their lives didn't speak of bravery and honor like the series tried to portray that my father found so interesting. They were in effect pagan, savages whose existence was soon brought to nothing by the spread of the glorious gospel of Christ.

By the year A.D. 1066, the Viking age had come to an end as their homeland of Scandinavia had been completely engulfed with Christianity.[31] The Vikings succumbed to the influence of the gospel. I can only imagine how miniscule their idea of bravery and courage must've sounded in comparison to the stories they were then being told of men and women suffering for the name of Jesus. Their idea of personal valor must've paled in comparison to what they were learning about Christians and how they were willing to die the death of criminals before committing the act of apostacy.

As I've stated, passion can sometimes cause us to overlook the facts. We're hit with the feeling of its appeal and immediately we run without ever considering the direction we're running. This man was holding to a belief or philosophy that died long ago. Maybe he chose to ignore the fact that the appeal of Christianity drew those men and women away from their pagan lifestyles and foolish barbarianism, or maybe he just didn't know. Well, to set the record straight, there's no belief or philosophical way of life more worthy of our heart's passion and complete devotion than our belief upon the glorious gospel of Jesus Christ. There may be a lot of things in this world to become passionate about, but none can compare to Him.

I hope this chapter will cause you to reflect upon where your passion has been channeled in your own personal life up until this point. As you reflect, I encourage you to refocus your energy and devotion upon Christ and His perfect will for your life. As you endeavor to develop your mane, directing your passion toward Christ and redirecting it away from the vanity of this world will be of the utmost importance.

We don't just come into manhood by happenstance. We become men because we purpose to let go of the things that only appeal to boys. It's the same with becoming a mature Christian who bears fruit unto the glory of God. We don't just suddenly arrive to maturity in Christ. It's when we purpose with all our heart to love God and conform to His ways that we begin to mature and develop. Mane-bearers have a single goal in life: to glorify God through our fruitful lives. Jesus said in John 15:8, "Herein is my Father glorified, that ye bear much fruit; so shall ye be my disciples."

Sometimes we think in order for our lives to bring God glory we have to do some great feat or accomplish some great achievement. But God has made honoring Him with our lives very simple; He says, "Bear much fruit." In lion language, that translates to, "Develop your mane." We want more than anything to be an asset to the Kingdom of God, but for us to become useful to God, we must prioritize Him and His will above our own. He must become our single passion in life.

All or Nothing

In 1997, Columbia Pictures produced a science fiction film entitled *Gattaca*, which told the story of Vincent Freeman, a man whose genetic traits were inferior to his genetically enhanced brother's. Vincent lived in a technologically advanced world that used reproductive technology and genetic engineering to enhance the physiological and psychological traits of mankind. People who were genetically modified were considered "Valids," while all others were considered "Invalids." Vincent was an Invalid, and what made matters worse was that his younger brother Anton was a Valid.

As is natural for brothers, Vincent and his younger brother grew up always competing against one another. They would go out to the ocean regularly and compete in a swimming competition between just the two of them. The rules were simple: the first to turn back to shore loses. As the years went by, Vincent, being the second-rate brother, would always lose to his artificially adept younger brother. He'd always be the first to turn back to shore.

That changed on one particular day when he and his brother set out for one final swim. The two brothers stepped off from shore and began their race as usual. Farther and farther they swam away from shore until they reached the distance Vincent would typically turn back, but Vincent showed no signs of quitting. To Anton's surprise, his brother continued the swim with Vincent out in the lead. By now, they had gone maybe double the distance they were accustomed to going and were a great way from shore.

Anton, wanting to turn back, called for Vincent and with great stress exclaimed, "What are you doing? How are you doing this? I can't see the shore anymore we have to turn back."

To this, Vincent asked, "Are you ready to quit?"

Anton replied, "No!" and they continued to swim.

After some more time, Anton caves and calls for Vincent once more, "Vincent! How are you doing this, Vincent? How have you done any of this? We have to go back. We have to save energy for the way back."

Vincent, looking at his younger brother as he treads water, responds, "You want to know how I did it? This is how I did it, Anton: I never saved anything for the swim back!"

You see, after years of losing and being counted as a failure, Vincent made up his mind that on that particular day he would succeed. He determined within his heart that if he had to die trying, he would beat his brother and prove that he was something in a world that only saw him as invalid. Through sheer human spirit and will, he determined in those moments before the race that life was not more valuable than passion, and brother, I want you to know that we too must come to this realization.

We too must be willing to pick up a passion worthy of our commitment, one whose rewards far outweigh all of the gains of life. A passion that, when brought into clear view, causes all other pursuits of the world to somehow decay in value and diminish in relevance. That passion, my friend, is that of the gospel of Jesus Christ.

Our passion for God must mean more to us than life itself. Isn't that the message of the gospel? Isn't that what Jesus taught when He said, "He that loseth his life for my sake shall find it" (Matthew 10:39)? Don't we see this passion-driven life exemplified in the life of Christ? Wasn't it Paul that said, "For to me to live is Christ, and to die is gain" (Philippians 1:21)? Didn't this same Paul say, "Neither count I my life dear unto me, so that I might finish my course with joy, and the ministry which I have received of the Lord Jesus, to testify of the gospel of the grace of God" (Acts 20:24)? Paul was about living for the Lord, and his life is our example.

It's all or nothing with God. There's not a such thing as a halfway Christian; our lives are either about Him or they're not. We're either living to please the Lord or we're living to please ourselves and the world. It's really that simple. Until we've understood this and we've begun to bear our cross and follow in the footsteps of our Savior, we will only appear to others as unpersuaded men, and I'll tell you, it's next to impossible to convince someone of something you're not convinced of yourself. It only comes across as powerless, ingenuine, and ultimately unappealing. If we're not passionate about the cross, we're passive about it, and passivity never saved a single soul from the snare of Satan.

Passion That Persuades

We must be careful to ensure that our passion for Christ and His great commission isn't only perceptible in the words we speak. It's easy to talk a good game. It takes little effort to develop the habit of being half religious and knowing how to talk religiously and make yourself appear to be something you're not. But God's intent isn't that we only appear as changed men, but that we are changed. Remember, He gets the glory when we bear much fruit. Our lives must prove that we are indeed passionate about Him and zealous about His will.

For the kingdom of God is not in word, but in power.

1 CORINTHIANS 4:20

Becoming a mane-bearer isn't about looking or sounding like someone you're not. It's not about putting energy into maintaining a certain image that doesn't accurately represent who you are at your core. Bearing a mane is about being a man who's zealous in permitting the Spirit of God to mold you from the inside out. It's about being humble and transparent with God, confessing to Him our weaknesses, and trusting Him to strengthen and develop us into men who glorify Him in every facet of our lives. We don't shy away from change; we welcome it. Walking with a mane mentality is about keeping yourself spotless from the world and faultless in all things. It's about putting on Christ and putting off self, because then and only then will we fulfill our God-given purpose to please Him and reach the lost before it's too late.

During his reign, King Solomon reaped the rewards of showing forth a heart that desired right things. At the onset of his reign, God made a promise to Solomon that He would reward him with riches and honor because his heart was in the right place. Solomon valued proper judgment and good understanding more than riches, and he pleased God as a result (1 Kings 3:10). It pleased Him so much that He gave Solomon the riches and honor he didn't ask for.

Word of King Solomon's splendor spread quickly, reaching the courts of queen Sheba. She heard rumor of his majesty and thought it couldn't be true. God had blessed the man so intensely that the news of his blessings seemed to the common mind unrealistic. In truth, it *was* unrealistic. Solomon wasn't blessed by any carnal means but by the hand of God, and that's why it was difficult for the queen of Sheba to accept the news that she was hearing. No king had ever been so endowed with wisdom and riches to her knowledge, so it seemed outlandish. But the idea of it sparked an intense interest in the queen's mind, and she wouldn't be satisfied until she went to see this great king and his kingdom with her own eyes.

And when the queen of Sheba had seen all Solomon's wisdom, and the house that he had built, and the meat of his table, and the sitting of his servants, and the attendance of his ministers, and their apparel, and his cup bearers, and his ascent by which he went up unto the house of the Lord; there was no more spirit in her. And she said to the king, It was a true report that I heard in my own land of thy acts and of thy wisdom. Howbeit I believed not the words until I came, and mine eyes had seen it.

1 KINGS 10:4-7

The queen was so stricken with awe and wonder at the sight of the king, the functioning of his kingdom, and the excellent manner of his leadership that the Bible says, "There was no more spirit in her." She might've fainted she was so overwhelmed by it all. She came as a questioning skeptic and left as a bona fide believer! She approached with a squinted eye of skepticism but departed with eyes of wonder! But it wasn't until she came and saw with her own eyes that she believed. The word of Solomon's unrivaled majesty wasn't enough for her to quietly trust in its validity. She needed hard evidence, and the same is true for the unbeliever today.

The word of our passion only is not enough to turn skeptics into believers; they need to *see* the hard evidence of our lives. They need hard evidence that our God is alive and active, presently working in our individual lives. They need to see with their own two eyes the wonders of God's mighty work in us. It's our faithfulness to the house of God and His work that they need to see when they peer into our lives. When the rains descend upon the just as they do the unjust, it's our unchanging joy and love for our God and others they need to witness. This is the sort of passion that persuades men to become believers. It's the power of the Holy Ghost living on the inside of us, working in us to darken the hue of our manes that causes the unbeliever to bust a U-ie and head in the direction of glory. The evidence they require is found in us, and it's when what's in us begins to come out of us that they, like Queen Sheba, lose spirit and begin to believe. Our passion for Christ is what will eventually persuade them to forsake all else and follow Him.

Blood-Stained Seeds

On November 25, 2006, Staff Sergeant Daniel Morris and his platoon set out for yet another convoy in the Diyala province just northeast of Bagdad, Iraq.[34] He had been on over three hundred combat missions prior to this one. As is standard for all convoys, the trucks were to be checked for proper maintenance, the troops were to be inspected by their leaders, and everyone was to be briefed on the purpose of the convoy prior to rolling out. Staff Sergeant Morris and his men were prepared for their next mission. While outside of the wire, patrolling their area of interest, Staff Sergeant Morris' Humvee struck a roadside improvised explosive device (IED), seriously wounding him and two of his comrades.

Prior to his deployment to Iraq, SSG Morris was described by his former pastor as being meek and quiet in character. He was thought of as having some degree of shyness, but everyone's perception of him changed on one particular day. His pastor recalled Staff Sergeant Morris vehemently rebuking a few of his troops one day for not reverencing the house of God. The quiet and soft-spoken brother had a depth to him that now was brought to light. His former pastor only then understood that his apparent shy and timid character was actually the fruit of a deep reverence for God and His house. He was passionate about God and nothing else fueled the fire he had on the inside. He had goals of attending Bible seminary after his military service and wanted to become a minister. Those goals were cut short the day of his death.

After the explosion, Staff Sergeant Morris' commander found him mortally wounded among the debris. As he began to assess his wounds, it was clear to both he and Staff Sergeant Morris that he wouldn't survive. His commander later told family members that before his passing Staff Sergeant Morris reached into his cargo pocket and handed him a Bible demanding that he give it to his father. He testified that Staff Sergeant Morris wasn't worried or fearful of the inevitable, but rather seemed to be at peace and ready for what was next. He recalled some of his last words being, "I'm going home now."

The commander stayed true to his word and ensured that the blood-stained Bible was presented to the soldier's father the day of his funeral ceremony. His father and several of his comrades later gave their life to Christ as a result of this man's great passion for the Lord. He could've requested his commander to tell his father a myriad of things during his last moments alive, but he simply handed him a Bible. He hoped that, after a life of devotion to the Lord, his war-torn Bible would be the final witness needed to save the soul of his dad. His father no doubt had already known about his son's life as a Christian, since his son would spend majority of his off time at his local church listening to sermons and fellowshipping with his pastor and fellow brothers and sisters, so he knew what sort of life his son lived. His father knew what his life was all about before he ever received that Bible. But when that commander approached him the day of his son's funeral it must've sent chills down his spine and tears down his face to know that his son's passion was true until the end.

It's one thing to profess our love for the Lord when life is warm and comfortable, but it's a completely different thing to say, "I love you, Lord," when all that's left of our lives are moments. SSG Morris' faith and passion for the Lord was true until the end.

This is the sort of passion and drive that won the hearts of the Vikings so long ago. It was the courage in battle and the will to fight until the end that they desired more than anything. It wasn't until they learned of One named Jesus that they understood what it really meant to never quit. It wasn't until they heard of the glorious gospel that their passion was redirected and their souls saved as a result.

When I heard Staff Sergeant Morris' pastor, who happened to be my pastor at the time, share the details of his life, my eyes began to fill with tears. The tears came when I learned that he left his Bible for his father and that his father had accepted his invitation to true salvation. I share the same hope of salvation for my father as SSG Morris did for his, and it's my hope that this chapter, even if but a little, nudges him towards the truth of the gospel. It's my hope that it nudges all men toward the love of God and the joy experienced in living a life that's all about Him in every way.

Eleven

The Keystone of America

*A father of the fatherless, and a judge of the widows, is God
in his holy habitation.*

PSALM 68:5

IN 1963, WORLD RENOWNED ECOLOGIST ROBERT PAINE made a discovery through a never done experiment that would change the world of ecology forever. Armed with just a crowbar and an unrelenting curiosity of nature, one by one Paine pried off an entire community of orange and purple starfish, also scientifically referred to as pisaster ochraceus and hurled them back into Mukkaw Bay.[35]

Up until this point, ecologists had only believed that animal population densities were determined primarily by the weather. It was the changes in temperature and precipitation frequency or infrequency that determined the overall animal structure and diversity of any given ecosystem. Paine wasn't convinced. Instead of accepting this notion, he set out to test a theory that animal communities and the diversity of the species that inhabit these communities were regulated by something else entirely.

To test this theory, he observed the effects of what would happen when he manually removed an entire community of starfish back into the bay, while leaving an adjacent community alone. Would the environment be altered in any way if he was to only take one species out of the picture? Did a single species have the power to change the overall functionality and balance of its environment by its presence or absence? Could it be that a single species would be so significant as to hold the key that would either cause an entire ecosystem to thrive or suffer?

These were questions Paine sought to answer through this simple yet never thought of experiment. The results proved to be groundbreaking with even Professor MacArthur, one of the leading ecologists at the time, after reviewing the seminal study published in 1966 saying, "This changes everything."[36]

After hurling the starfish back into the bay and observing the environment following their absence, Paine watched in wonder as the ecosystem began to transform right before his eyes.

Ochre Starfish are predatory creatures that prey on algae, crustaceans, and limpets among other species that live along the rocky coast. They're the first species to be given the title keystone because of the significant role they play in their ecosystem. Paine coined the term "keystone species" based off the centerpiece located at the apex of an archway, a piece that's necessary to provide stability to the entire structure. When this piece is removed from the arch, it causes all the other stones to fall. When he removed the starfish from their environment, this allowed opportunity for other species which the starfish would prey on to increase in number, thus altering the environment.

Within only three months of the experiment, Paine observed one prey species known as acorn barnacles begin to occupy sixty to eighty percent of the now available space. After a year of observation, four species of algae had completely disappeared due to the increase in crustaceans which prey upon the algae. With the starfish now out of the way, its ecosystem was beginning to shift dramatically. Sean B. Carroll, a professor of molecular biology and genetics at the University of Wisconsin-Madison said in his book, *The Serengeti Rules: The Quest to Discover How Life Works and Why It Matters,* "Altogether, the removal of the predatory starfish had quickly reduced the diversity of the intertidal community from the original fifteen species to eight."[37]

It was the presence of the starfish that kept several species at bay, which in turn protected other species such as those of the algae family from predatory interactions. Paine's discovery of the effects of what happens when a keystone species is removed from its ecosystem is now commonly referred to as "Kick It and See" ecology.

Kick It and See

Prior to the industrial revolution period ranging from 1800 to the mid 1900s, the average American family consisted of both a father and a mother. During the early 1800s, at least three quarters of the American workforce were engaged in agricultural work, which meant families were together day in and day out, collectively addressing the demands of running the farm. Remember, less time equals less influence, while more time means just the opposite. During the infancy stages of American history, fathers were home for majority of the day. It was common for fathers to be completely involved in the rearing of their children and the overall affairs of the home. Fathers were adept managers of their own homes taking a personal interest in the schooling, character development, and spiritual competence of their families.

Consider what David Blankenhorn has to say on the issue in his book *Fatherless America,* "Most important, fathers assumed primary responsibility for what was seen as the most essential parental task: the religious and moral education of the young. As a result, societal praise or blame for a child's outcome was customarily bestowed not (as it is today) on the mother but on the father." He continues, "The nineteenth century's progressive fragmentation of labor, combined with mass production and complicated administration, the separation of home and the place of work, [and} the transition from independent producer to paid employee who uses consumer goods led to a progressive loss of substance of the father's authority and diminution of his power in the family and over the family."[38]

Prior to this cataclysmic and destructive change to the American family, it was generally conceived that fathers were the primary influencers of the family, and in cases of divorce, fathers were almost always granted custody of the children. Dad was in fact the center of the home. He was the one thing that ensured the family was moving in the right direction. He was the keystone of the family unit – the piece that kept everything and everyone joined together. That all changed at the onset of the industrial revolution.

As factories were beginning to erect in major cities like New York, Philadelphia, and Chicago, the demand for men to work in those factories became increasingly high. This resulted in families packing their belongings and heading for the big city. Mothers had no choice but to take up the primary responsibility of the family as their husbands would now spend 14 to 16 hours a day in the factory. This was an incredibly significant change to the functionality of the American family and would inevitably have adverse effects. America soon saw what happened when husbands and fathers were kicked almost completely out of the home.

Paine's experiment and discovery of the keystone species sent shockwaves throughout the entire ecological community, causing ecologists to experiment with other species. There was now a fiery interest in the possibility of discovering other keystones throughout the many ecosystems of the world. If starfish could have such an immense impact on their ecosystem, what of other species?

Lion numbers have been on the decline for quite some time now. They've suffered at the hand of local farmers due to their natural interest in livestock, and their numbers have dwindled as a result of the ever-increasing popularity of trophy hunting. It's difficult to imagine a world where lions can only be viewed as moldings at amusement parks and museum exhibits displayed right beside the tyrannosaurus rex. Can you imagine taking your little one to the museum and, upon seeing a depiction of a stuffed lion pouncing on a buffalo, your child asks, "Daddy, what's that?" Though it may be difficult to imagine such a reality, the fact is that the king of beasts is heading in the direction of the dinosaur.

The National Geographic estimates less than 25,000 lions remaining in Africa today, which is about half their population from 25 years ago.[39] With numbers so few, lions have been listed as vulnerable to extinction by the International

Union for the Conservation of Nature, which determines the conservation status of species. So, what happens when a keystone species as significant as the lion disappears from its environment? Do things just continue as they were? Well, to put it simple, if the lion is gone, the grass of the open plains is consumed a lot faster and other animal herds become weaker, which causes a cascading effect across all the savannah.

Lions are considered keystone because they provide a stability to the savannah that, if hindered, would cause a major shift in the environment's overall balance. Mufasa was on to something when he made mention of the circle of life. Lions prey on the herbivores that eat the grass of the plains. Their predation regulates the amount of vegetation that's consumed by herbivores. Lions are also well known for being opportunists; they prefer to prey on the weak and sickly among the herds as they are typically the easiest to catch. If lions were removed from their environment, herbivores would overwhelm the plant life bringing famine to all plant eaters. The lions' absence would enable disease to spread throughout the herds as they would no longer be available to remove the sickly, thus causing a decline in other animal's population numbers. Their presence in the savannah is needed to provide balance to the food supply as well as to prevent the spread of disease. Their presence prevents famine and disease!

In much the same way, the role of dark-maned husbands, fathers, and men in our homes and communities across our nation is essential to the prevention of spiritual famine and disease. We need the presence of godly men in our homes and communities if we're to maintain a balance of righteousness, good judgment, and equity throughout our nation and lineages. Without the presence of a righteous man, the bread of life is scarcely found, and the disease of sinfulness is left to spread far and wide without hindrance.

The moment we regulate the role of a godly man as the head of our American families to something optional is the moment the gears of terribleness begin to turn. But that's exactly what has happened. American society has begun to move in a direction away from God. We've reduced the image and description of a man to something weak and passive, thus causing the need for his presence to be seen as something unnecessary. If men are thought of as weak and meagerly, then what need do we have of them anymore? If men aren't bearing their responsibility of manhood with pride and resolve, then let's just put a woman in his place and redefine the family. Brother, this is the reality we're faced with today. This is the big buffalo standing in our way.

There was a very popular cartoon series that aired on television when I was a kid back in the 90s called *Rugrats*. To give you the quick rundown, if you're not already familiar, the show pictured talking baby characters that would go on wild excursions that consisted primarily of their imagination. The parents of these children were always in some fashion preoccupied with either business, social gatherings, or personal interests, so it made it easy for the children to wander off into their own little imaginative world.

When the show originally aired, Phil and Lil, a set of toddler twins on the show, both shared parents Howard and Betty DeVille. Betty and Howard didn't exemplify a traditional marriage on the original show with Betty being the more dominant of the two and Howard being a stay-at-home dad that was very much afraid of his overly domineering wife.

However unorthodox their marriage was, the two were still married. In the reboot, however, Howard is taken completely out of the picture, and Betty is openly a lesbian. Remember, this show was originally intended for the eyes of young people, but the reboot carries a trace of modernism clearly designed to appeal to millennials. Fifty years ago, such a show would have never been aired or even thought of for that matter. This is only one example of how removed our society has become, that entertainment mediums such as that of television and children's literature are now attempting to normalize ungodliness.

The family structure has changed dramatically since the days prior to the industrial revolution. Children are now being adopted by people of the same sex and they're calling it a family. People are going to the courts and making it official in the world's eyes, but God hasn't changed and neither has His position on the family structure.

God doesn't acknowledge the joining of man and man or woman and woman as anything other than sin. There's nothing holy about it. No matter how much the people of this world try to pervert the family unit, no matter how much they try and create their own idea of what a family is, they can't deny it when they see an actual family by God's design. There's something pure and right about a man and a woman holding hands as they stroll through the mall or the park with their children. There's a natural purity affixed to the image of a biblical family that burns itself into the conscience of those who live contrary to it.

Just as the lion has been attacked over the years and their numbers have suffered as a result, so men have undergone much scrutiny and adversarial pursuit. Satan has a fiendish goal of perverting the image of the man and removing him altogether from every family and home. Somewhere dark and cruddy, there's the phrase, "Do away with the man!", written in bold ink underlined in red marker on a yellow sticky note at the center of Satan's corkboard. God's man has always been a threat to the devil's kingdom since the dawn of life here on earth. It was Satan who laid the hazard in the way for man to trip and fall an eternal fall. It was Satan who influenced the heart of Pharoah to do away with all the Hebrew boys at the beginning of Moses' life. Satan foresaw the exodus of Israel and no doubt attempted to prevent it long before it began. But God made a way, as He always does. It was Satan who influenced the heart of king Herod when he issued the order to have all of the boys two years and under in Bethlehem killed. Again, Satan was attempting to murder the Messiah before He would have opportunity to save and empower man. It was that old serpent, the devil, influencing the heart and momentum behind the early persecution of the Church, which saw thousands of men martyred for their faith in Christ. And it's Satan behind today's push for policies that support abortion; it's Satan behind the self-focused and self-consumed mentality that many men have today. It's Satan, my friend, who's behind the passive approach many men take toward living for God.

True Bible-believing and Bible-living Christians are often the subject of cruel and oppressive scrutiny because of the manner in which we live our lives. I must preface the term Christian the way I did because of how often Christianity is misrepresented today. To others, our modest apparel and moderate lives are viewed as "too much" or seen as some form of bondage. Many people who profess to know God have become so accustomed to modern society and popular trends that pure biblical teachings and examples are seen as outlandish and therefore abhorred in their sight.

Someone very close to me was approached by a professing Christian family member and asked if they were in a cult based solely on the appearance of her apparel, which was totally pure and modest. The fact that she had chosen to forsake wearing clothing that revealed and accentuated her body was a cause of concern for the professing Christian who had asked the question. But shouldn't she had rather applauded her for her chaste life? Shouldn't she had rather thanked God that her close relative wasn't bowing down to those societal norms that approve of nakedness? Shouldn't she had rather sang praises unto God for the obedience that her loved one was now demonstrating in turning away from a spirit of lasciviousness? I'd say yes, but there are those that have drifted away from the simplicity of Scripture and so what is right is always seen as something wrong from their worldly perspective. They're not finding fault with the lives of true Christians, ultimately; they're finding fault with God and with His Word.

They say that purposing to be in the house of God several days a week is unnecessary, that Sunday morning is enough to carry one through the week. But we understand that Scripture reveals a necessity for the house of the Lord in the life of all who profess to follow Him. We acknowledge that if we're to develop our manes and exemplify a life of fruitfulness, we will have to establish roots within the confluence of God's house. They say that it's okay to watch what you want and listen to whatever kind of music you prefer to listen to without considering the content. But we've learned through

Scripture that it's our responsibility to become selective eaters and that God expects us to monitor our spiritual food intake and partake of only what is pure. They disapprove of our chaste life because they're unwilling themselves to give their hearts over completely to God. Satan is behind such men and women that toe the line of sin and worldliness regardless of what they profess. Jesus said, "By their fruits you shall know them." And it's their lack of fruit and their scruffy manes that prove to us that their suggestions to live a non-biblical life is influenced by none other than Satan himself. Satan is so viciously determined to do away with God's man that he'll resort to infiltrating God's Church through the lives of men and women who have a form of godliness but deny the power thereof. Satan's terribly bent on doing away with God's man.

But so long as God has men, He will not succeed. God will always have men. So long as there are a few dark manes patrolling the territory of their families and communities, Satan will cower in fear and frustration. We must stand our ground! So long as we're willing to be men of risk and risk the destruction of our worldly reputations, Satan will have nothing to stand on. We must realize that like the lions of the savannah, the man of God that bears fruit is the keystone of his family and community, and ultimately of our great nation. It's when we remove him or he removes himself from his intended place of leadership and influence that a breakdown of our families, communities, and nation begins.

The American Nightmare

One of the impacts of men spending more time away from home during the industrial period was the loss of focus upon the family. Men were no longer as concerned with the affairs of their homes as they once were, and it can be easy to understand why. They were spending far less time with their wives and children, which meant that their time and energy were being exhausted either on the job or in some leisure activity. Fathers were no longer as concerned with the educational and spiritual wellness of their families, but now had an inordinate interest in the new idea of an American dream.

America struck gold in its new economic development, with products now being mass produced. Families were now flocking to the cities where their husbands were working their new factory jobs. Businessmen were beginning to see opportunity in this new influx of people and thus was born electronic advertisement mediums such as that of the television and radio during this period. Owning the latest car on the market and a house on the hills became every man's dream. Men wanted to portray in their own lives the image of success that was then being depicted through the media. The idea of tangible success became a common desire and pursuit, to the point where men worked long hours at the expense of their families to achieve it. This new idea of the American dream, no doubt, seemed the way to go for many men during that era, as all of the Western world was moving in that direction.

The world often tries to persuade us to follow in the way of popularity. They say there must be some validity to it if everyone is doing it, right? But God says just the opposite. He commands us not to follow the trends of this world no matter how many others are walking in that way. He calls us to go against the grain of life, to march to a different beat, to walk in *The Way of the Mane*!

This new idea of the American dream resulted in just the opposite of what was being strived for. Ironically enough, the

American dream our great grands once pursued proved to be a nightmare when we examine the impact it has had on our society as a whole. Today's prisons and mental asylums are filled with men and women who have and still do feel the effects of having to negotiate life apart from a father. These effects are felt primarily because dad took more interest in the car he drove than in the welfare of his own children. We see the impact of fatherlessness every time a video of young people fighting in the streets is streamed on our newsfeeds, every time we see young women dressed provocatively in public settings, and with every ill-mannered encounter we come across with young people today.

I recently came across a story of a teenage girl who was shot several times by a police officer. The officer was alerted by a dispatch of a teenager attempting to stab another person, and he immediately drove to the location. Upon arrival, bodycam footage shows a group of teenagers brawling in the front lawn of a house with one of the young girls wielding a knife. The officer opens fire when the young girl lunges at another, evidently attempting to inflict bodily harm. The young girl died as a result of her gunshot wounds.

Much outrage was directed toward the officer who fired the shots when the news spread. Many offered their opinions of how they thought the officer should have responded differently in that situation. They said he fired too many shots. They said he should have aimed his weapon in a nonlethal area of the girl's body. They said he should be charged with murder, and I'm sure we can sit and discuss for hours on in how the officer might've done things differently to achieve a better result, but in fact, the officer acted within his legal authority to protect another defenseless individual.

While many were pointing their fingers at the officer as the subject of blame for the girl's untimely death, no one ever thought to consider the background of the child as a contributing and, might I add, substantial element of the entire situation. No one ever considered the picture as a whole; it was only the stain at the center that caught everyone's attention. No one thought to ask where the children's parents were while they were brawling in the streets.

It turns out that the young girl was a foster child and was accustomed to defending herself for much of her life. She had been diverted to the foster system because her mother was not fit to care for her and her grandmother had lost custody of her after being evicted from her home. Her father had scarcely been involved in her life and certainly wasn't present on the day she needed him the most.

The truth is that the likelihood of those children fighting in the streets had there been a present and active father in their lives would've been slim to none. There were, from my memory, only two men seen in the video: the police officer and a participating member of the brawl, which might I remind you involved children. There was no authoritative male figure there to provide some degree of left and right limitations and so things got out of hand.

You see, a father's presence alone demands a certain standard of behavior; there are things we just don't do in the presence of our fathers. But it can be that a father possesses the power even to occupy himself within the heart and mind of his child while he may not even be physically present. This is only true if he's put in the work beforehand.

Being a father isn't as difficult as others might portray; it's really as simple as showing up and being present. But this has been understood by our adversary the devil and so it's our presence that he attempts to strip from our families. If we're not working, we're out on the green putting for par. If we're not golfing, we're waist deep in a fresh-water stream with our buddies trying to hook a fish. If we're not fishing, we're under a bar pushing 225 at the gym. If we're not at the gym, we're intensely staring and yelling back into a rectangular piece of plastic and glass, playing video games. If we're not...well, you understand what I'm saying.

How often do you ask your buddy his plans for the weekend and he tells you something lame like, "Taking my kids to the playground," or "Taking my family on a fishing trip"? It's not very often. Men typically think of spending time with their families as something mandatory that must be satisfied so that we can do all the other things I mentioned without feeling guilty. It's typically not our preference. Until we make our families our preference and priority, Satan will continue to succeed in his tactic of stripping our families of our presence.

Your presence is a point of concern to him because, if you remember, testosterone is a terrible deterrent to thievery! So, that feeling you get in your heart when your wife asks you to stay home and spend time with her and the kids when you have your mind set on something else must not be suppressed but rather recognized and purposefully silenced. It's an internal war that you must wage against yourself and the enemy of your soul if you are to have any righteous influence over your pride. But as in this young girl's case, when dad's interests lie elsewhere, Satan will find the breach in security and exploit it every time.

Where was dad while all this chaos was going on? He was nowhere to be found. There wasn't a present man, father, or father figure there to patrol that young girl's life, and so the enemy of her soul found the breach and exploited it. How many more tragedies do we have to witness before we realize that men of character, men of extraordinary faith in Christ, men that are zealous of good works are needed now more than ever before?

This American nightmare has been in development for multiple decades now. If I were to show you a column graph of the percentage of fatherlessness from 1960 to present, you'd immediately notice a progressive increase in fatherless homes over the past sixty years. The keystone of America's absence has just about tripled since 1960 with close to one in four children living without present fathers today.[40] This means that nearly a quarter of all children currently living in America are going to bed and awakening every day to fatherless homes. This means that nearly a quarter of all American children will grow up under the influence of external sources outside of their homes, such as that of mainstream media and rotten apples as opposed to that of a father. Close to a fourth of our children will never know what it feels like to live with a healthy reverence and fear of a father, which is able to save them from so much.

During fellowship one evening, the topic of discourse somehow made its way to fatherhood. One of the brothers began to explain his upbringing, expressing to us his relationship with his father when he was a teenager. He made mention to various popular and yet unethical activities he had every opportunity to take part in, but as he expressed, "I withheld myself because I feared my dad." I found this very interesting since I had never experienced such convictions as a teen. I had never paused to consider what my father might do to me or how disappointed he might become as a result of my actions...simply because he wasn't around. The degree to which he was present wasn't enough to instill in me a sense of reverence for him. It wasn't like I was going home to a big burly man waiting at the door anticipating my arrival. My father was across town fully plunged into his own interests.

However, I did stop to consider the whooping I would receive from my mother had she ever discovered my disobedience, but that consideration was not grave enough to cause me to halt my juvenile rebellion. I remember as a boy weighing the consequences of my actions and actually envisioning my mother's belt against my hide, somewhat feeling the pain of it as if I were there already. But the folly was so bound up in my heart that I thought it was worth it and would proceed to commit the offence. Eventually, I'd grow into a young man and those moments of self-preserving forethought would cease. It didn't matter to me what my mother would do anymore. I was more man than boy in terms of stature, and my mother had no doubt grown weary of shepherding me alone for all those years.

While I appreciate my mother's commitment to raising and disciplining me, I understand that it was the presence of my father I was lacking. It was the image of that broad-shouldered man that I needed in the back of my mind that would've likely curbed my behavior and caused me to maybe consider the ramifications of my actions for a little longer.

You see, a boy needs to know that when he returns home there will be a man waiting there that's madly devoted to holding him accountable for his actions. He needs to know that this man not only rules with a rod of iron but also with a heart of intense love for him. He must understand that there is a standard of behavior that his father expects him to up-hold, and if he ever thinks to allow the youthful madness within his heart to unleash, he is taking a very grave risk. But when dad isn't even in the picture, and there's no man stand-ing at the end of the driveway waiting for Jimmy to come home, Jimmy may not even come home. Jimmy may wander off after school and find something to get into. When Jimmy's friends shove a bottle of alcohol into his chest or pass a blunt his way, Jimmy may pause for one significant moment to consider his mother. But the pressure will be too heavy, the temptation too hot, and the consequence not grave enough to refuse. Jimmy's first encounter with real peer pressure will result in failure, and there will be nothing in his way prevent-ing him from future failures.

There are a lot of boys like Jimmy in our country today that, because of the absence of their fathers, have wondered off and found something to get into. I have friends and close loved ones that fit the description of Jimmy and I'm sure you do too. I was a Jimmy at one point in my life, but that all changed when I came to know Jesus and began to experience His presence and power.

A father of the fatherless, and a judge of the widows, is God in his holy habitation.

PSALM 68:5

Of the many wonderful promises God gives to His chil-dren, the promise of fathering us must ranks pretty high. In a day and age when men are abandoning their own children more than ever, this promise from our Heavenly Father reassures us of our future. It assures us that we don't have to be orphans any longer and that we don't even have to resent our earthly fathers anymore. God says, "You are now mine," and that should be enough for us to rise from our sunken existence and walk in newness of life.

We must be of the mindset that if no one else will arise to the standard of righteousness God expects of us, we will. No longer can we waddle in despair over the state of our current society, but the time has come for us to be the keystone our families, communities, and country needs. It does no one any good to simply talk about the problems we all see without putting forth any action to resolve them. It's easy to identify problems especially when they're as prevalent as they are today. But what's not easy is making a personal decision to stop waiting on the change and to stand up and *be* the change!

This is what we need. We need men like you and me to decide within the secrecy of our hearts that we're going to be all that God has designed us to be. If we fail to choose wisely and choose rather to continue in our slumber mesmerized by the vanities of a false American dream, we will only perpetuate the life of the nightmare that is presently destroying our nation.

Twelve

The Mane Point

*Then saith he unto his disciples, The harvest truly is
plenteous, but the labourers are few.*

– MATTHEW 9:37

O N MAY 9, 2021, MY AND MY WIFE'S LIVES WERE CHANGED
in the most extraordinary way. It was a typical Sunday.
We spent the morning celebrating Mother's Day and wor-
shipping God at our church with close friends. After fellowshipping, we came home and rested all afternoon until it was
time for us to go back to service that evening. Once the time
came, we all loaded inside our vehicle and headed for evening service. While in route, about half a mile from the exit
where our church was located, my wife inhaled sharply and
shouted, "Andre! Watch out!"

I looked out of my driver side window and saw a Ford Ex-
plorer traveling on the opposite side of traffic cross the grassy
highway median, lose control, and roll several times about
three meters away from our vehicle. I quickly pulled the vehicle over to the right side of the highway, my vision completely blocked by the dirt, rocks, and dust the vehicle had

kicked up as it rolled. I put the vehicle in park, opened my door, and began to sprint through the debris that lay spread across the roadway, heading for the crashed vehicle. As I went, I began to exclaim, "Jesus! Jesus! Jesus! Help me, Lord!"

The vehicle was destroyed. Broken parts of the truck spread on both sides of the highway, causing traffic to come to a complete halt. The vehicle had landed right side up after rolling three times. As I peered around the corner of the front of the vehicle, I remember hoping the driver had somehow made it out unscathed. I was afraid of what I might find in that driver's seat after such a devastating crash. A few more steps, and I found a young man unconscious, his extremities contorted in an unnatural way, and as I placed two of my fingers upon his carotid artery, I felt no pulse. A quick glance to the ground beneath the crushed vehicle revealed a liquid of some sort coming from beneath the crushed hood. I immediately thought it to be fuel. I rushed forward, signaling all on-coming traffic to back up fearing the vehicle might catch fire at any moment.

I heard a voice across the crash zone and saw a middle-aged woman handling what I thought, in the moment, to be a severed body part, but when I looked more keenly, I noticed another young man laying among the debris. I hadn't been aware of the other victim. He had been ejected from the vehicle. His broken body was hidden among all the debris, and I had run right passed him. She was calling for me to assist her. I quickly ran over to provide her whatever aid I could. She seemed to have some experience as a medical professional. I ran and knelt at the victim's side with her. He was also unconscious. I could hear him struggling to breathe as his body lay limp on its side. We turned him from his side to his back, tore off his t-shirt, and searched his body for any visible wounds other than his obvious head injury. We found none except for a sign of internal bleeding at the center of his chest.

By this time, a firemen's crew had arrived which had to have been less than 10 minutes after the accident. They quickly took over, providing an oxygen mask to the man that had been ejected from the vehicle and checking for a pulse from the driver. They encouraged us to continue to reassure the ejected victim that everything would be okay. I placed my hand upon his chest, offering him reassuring words, unsure if he could even hear me.

While they continued to tend to his needs, I went and retrieved my cellphone from the grass on the side of the highway. I had tossed it as a precaution upon sighting the fuel leaking form the vehicle. I returned to the young man lying in the road, placed my hand upon his leg, and began to pray in the Spirit as well as in English. After praying earnestly for about a minute and seeing that my assistance was no longer needed, I returned to my vehicle where my wife stood at the trunk with tears in her eyes, praying for the two young men involved in the accident. We left and soon arrived at our church, still very much moved by it all. We prayed together before service, thanking the Lord for protecting us and shielding us from being hit by the vehicle as it rolled. We prayed for the young men as their lives still lay in the balance, and we proceeded to sing praises to God as service began.

Reality Check

Following the accident, my wife and I both talked about how we felt as everything was transpiring. We both could attest to a severe tenderness of heart and mind that wasn't as keen before our brush with death. It was as if nothing else mattered in that short span of time except our labors for the Lord and where we each stood with Him at that present time. Were we doing enough to reach the lost for Christ? In addition to this, a great sense of responsibility for the souls of men and women came over us as we witnessed two lives suddenly being cut off. We weren't thinking about what we were to eat for dinner that evening following service. We weren't concerned with how much money we had in our bank account or any other facet of our finances. There came no thought or mental attentiveness to our plans for the future and ambitions. Nothing of worldly value occupied our minds, and there was no thought of materialism among the traffic of thoughts within our mental activity. Only the reality that two men were in a very bad way and the question of their souls' condition lingered with us. Unsure of whether the two men were able to make it out alive, I searched for a news report on the accident the next day and learned that both men died that very same night only three hours apart.

This was a reality check for us. This was a traumatic experience in which two men lost their lives suddenly. This was a misfortune in which two mothers lost two sons on Mother's Day. We grieved with the surviving family members while simultaneously corralling together as a family, thankful for the Lord's protection. We're thankful that the Lord allowed us to witness the crash without harm or suffering, because in our witnessing, more fuel has been pumped into our passion for reaching the lost. Our perspective upon life and our calling has become purer as a result of what our eyes have seen.

It's as if the Lord allowed us a glimpse into what He sees every day. He sees men and women dying, lost in their sins around the clock, and He wants something to be done about it. The Bible tells us that our God is not willing that any should perish but that all should come to repentance (2 Peter 3:9). The God we know and love has no desire for people to die lost, but He sees it every day. He witnesses thousands upon thousands of the souls of men and women dying separate from Him every day, and His heart weeps for them. Our hearts became more tender as a result of the crash, but the Lord's heart is always tender. He's constantly in a state of deep concern for those who wander lost. He's always moved by the wandering of the masses.

But when he saw the multitudes, he was moved with compassion on them, because they fainted, and were scattered abroad, as sheep having no shepherd. Then saith he unto his disciples, The harvest truly is plenteous, but the labourers are few; Pray ye therefore the Lord of the harvest, that he will send forth labourers into his harvest.

MATTHEW 9:36-38

This is the reality we all must come to grips with. The world we live in, overwhelming, is comprised of lost men and women who desperately need a Savior to save them from their sins and give them a better direction in life, a direction that leads to redemption through Christ. Because the current of life moves in a direction opposite of righteousness, there has now fallen a calling from God upon the shoulders of men. This calling demand that we unhesitatingly put away our selfish attitudes and interests and that we put on the new man fashioned after Christ. This calling requires a certain gall and grit within our hearts. It requires a measure of spiritual testosterone and tenacity to buck up against Satan's kingdom. It necessitates a pure understanding of the world around us and, with this holy understanding, a resolve to labor with and for the Lord.

Notice the words of the Savior, "The harvest truly is plenteous, but the laborers are few." What did He mean by this? Had He briefly fastened His eyes on a local garden or vineyard nearby? What exactly was Jesus saying here? Since the day He commissioned the disciples to follow Him and to put away their personal occupations, Jesus hadn't lost His focus. His vision was just as clear before as it was then as He stood looking on a multitude of people with the eyes and heart of tender compassion. Jesus was saying to the men who followed Him that the lost souls of men were in abundance and that there were only few willing to labor in the fields of life. There were only a few who had such an enlightened understanding of life that would cause them to see the multitude as anything other than a large mass of people. Jesus saw more than just a large mass of people, He saw opportunity!

What do you see when you peer into the world around you? When you look out into the lives of men and women all around, what exactly do you see? Do you only see people carrying on with their lives and think nothing of it? Or do you see a vast field just waiting to be harvested? Do you see opportunity?

That's what this book has been about. It's been about possessing the fruit and vision needed to make a real and eternal impact in the world around us. That's what I want you to gain from reading this. I want you to leave these pages understanding that God desires for you to become a laborer with and for Him and that, for you to be effective in your service to Him, you must possess fruit. I pray that the eyes of your understanding are enlightened to the reality of life. I pray that this book has been a reality check for you. I pray that you experience the pureness of perspective that comes from knowing the Savior and aligning your ways with His.

Jesus is looking for laborers as is evident in the text we just read. But in order to be a laborer for the Lord and for it to mean something, we first must be made usable. This means that our old heart, our old mentality, and ultimately our old self must be done away with, and we must become new creatures in Him. Many men have attempted to work for the Lord without first being changed and made new, and this only results in a powerless and ingenuine effort. God must change us and give us a new heart that desires new things first because then we won't labor reluctantly or grudgingly or insincerely. It'll be out of a real passion and zeal for Him and His calling.

Becoming a Laborer

At the onset of my walk with God, back when I didn't have the slightest idea of what Christianity was all about and what it meant to follow the Lord, I learned a very valuable lesson about how to begin with God. I was in my late teens when there came an urgency within my heart to live differently than I had been accustomed to up until that point. I knew it was time for a change. Though I didn't understand or even have the slightest idea of what would come of the changes I was to make, I knew that the source of this urgency came from God, and so I gave it my attention. I knew He was trying to communicate with me to get me moving in the direction of life, and so I did something I had never done before. I began to pray earnestly for the first time in my life.

For the first time in my life, I allowed my soul to cry out unto God and I began to express all my worries, fears, concerns, and desires. This wasn't just a one-time thing where I prayed once and that was it. I set my heart to seek the Lord and I began to pray consistently everyday, trying earnestly to make a connection with Him. I learned then that, like radio communications, if the signal is strong enough and your antenna is pointed in the right direction, you will hit your mark! It was during this time of personal devotion to God that I began to hear from Him, and thus His work had begun within me.

Being confident of this very thing, That he which hath begun a good work in you will perform it until the day of Jesus Christ.

PHILIPPIANS 1:6

In order to become a laborer with and for the Lord, you must allow Him to begin His work within you. You may be wondering, "Well how do I do that?" It's never as complicated as we or others make it out to be. It's as simple as beginning on your knees in humble and earnest prayer. This is our rightful place as men. The Bible tells us that when Jesus discovered that He was fashioned after the likeness of man, He immediately humbled Himself and became obedient to the will of God (Philippians 2:8). I love this scripture because it reveals to us man's most proper disposition: humility. While the world would have us think that prayer has no significance and it can yield no real results, I'm here to tell you that's the biggest lie anyone has ever told. We begin with God by humbling ourselves and communicating with Him through prayer. There is no other way!

If my people, which are called by my name, shall humble themselves, and pray, and seek my face, and turn from their wicked ways; then will I hear from heaven, and will forgive their sin, and will heal their land.

2 CHRONICLES 7:14

This is the blueprint, brother. If there are any secret sins within your life that only you and God know about, it's time for you to humble yourself and follow this guide back to right-standing with God. So many people today within the religious community think they can continue living a sinful life and that God will somehow overlook their offenses. This is not how God operates. The Bible very clearly paints a portrait of a God who abhors sin, and it tells us that it's because of our sins that we become separate from Him (Isaiah 59:2). We permit Him to begin His work in our lives when we follow the blueprint laid out for us in 2 Chronicles 7:14. We welcome Him into our lives and permit Him to make the changes He deems as necessary when we not only accept Him and communicate with Him, but when we also follow His instructions and do what He's wanting us to do.

This is how the great men of old began to walk with God. The Apostle Paul's relationship with God began on his knees, and it continued to flourish by reason of His obedience to the Lord's instructions. Moses' extraordinary walk with God began with him humbling himself and following simple instructions to go into a place he probably had made up in his mind he would never return. But it didn't matter what he had predetermined in his mind, because it was the Lord speaking.

The Apostle Peter's walk with the Lord, too, began on his

knees. He and his friends had been laboring all night trying to catch some fish when Jesus came requesting to use his ship as a speaking platform. After Jesus had finished addressing the multitude, He commanded Peter to thrust the ship out further into the deep and to let down his nets for a draught. To this, Peter offered his rebuttal but obeyed, nonetheless.

And Simon answering said unto him, Master, we have toiled all the night, and have taken nothing: nevertheless at thy word I will let down the net. And when they had done this they inclosed a great multitude of fishes: and their net brake. And they beckoned unto their partners, which were in the other ship, that they should come and help them. And they came, and filled both ships, so that they began to sink. When Simon Peter saw it he fell down at Jesus' knees, saying, Depart from me; for I am a sinful man, O Lord.

LUKE 5:5-8

Peter would go on to follow Jesus, witnessing and personally experiencing the power of God. He would be commissioned by Christ to lead the early Church. But the same that was true for Paul, for Moses, and for Peter must be true for us. We must begin on our knees in humility before God, exclaiming with all sincerity of heart, "Lord, what would thou have me to do?" And if our journey with the Lord must begin on our knees, we can be sure that it must continue there.

These men learned what God wanted them to do for Him when they came to Him with humble hearts in prayer. Their labors for and with God hadn't begun until after they humbled themselves, prayed, and followed His instructions. The work of the Lord began in their hearts the moment they came to Him in humility.

Notice too, that of the three men I mentioned, each of them had seemingly legitimate excuses as to why they shouldn't have been called by God. Paul was a persecutor of the Church and, by his own admission, the chief of all sinners. Moses had killed a man in the land God was instructing him to return. He also had a speech impediment which would seem reasonable enough for God to reconsider sending him to speak to a king. But God wasn't depending on Moses' ability to deliver His people or His message; He was sure of His own. Finally, the Apostle Peter did not hesitate to confess to Jesus that he was a sinful man, unworthy of the Lord's presence. But the Lord called him, nonetheless.

You see, if God is desiring to begin a work in us, then the implication is that we need to be worked on. Why would He begin a work on someone who thinks he's already where he needs to be? Even we don't fix things that don't have a need to be fixed. We fix what is broken so that we can use it again. God is the same way. He doesn't begin a work in us and fix us so we can sit by idle. What good is a broken chair when it is fixed if no one sits in it? If it wasn't going to be used by anyone, it could've remained broken. In like manner, God begins His work in us with a purpose in mind. He wants a return on His investment. His desire is that, once His work has begun within us and He has fixed the broken areas of our being, we would go and do the same for others through the power He provides. We then become His hands and feet. He wants us to eventually become laborers for and with Him to reach the lost souls of men and women whom He loves so very intensely.

So, the first step in becoming a laborer for the Lord is to begin in humble and earnest prayer, and the second is like unto it: continue in humble and earnest prayer and heed the Lord's instructions.

A Putting Down and a Picking Up

When I was about eight years old, I inadvertently discovered one of my father's pornographic VHS tapes. I don't remember how it came into my possession, but I can tell you of the internal war that ensued as a result of me finding it. From that moment forward, pornography became what I'd call a secret sin in my life only I knew about – or so I thought. As the years went by, this new-found pleasure became increasingly more difficult to break away from, primarily because I hadn't developed a desire to be free. I knew, in moments of frustration and unease, I could turn to this habit and temporarily escape from the woes of my existence. It was as if I had stumbled upon a hot coal in the way and, unable to perceive the potential of its danger, I decided to pick it up, put it in my pocket, and began to handle it against reason.

After many years of being burned as a boy, I found myself as a married man and father to a young girl, shamefully admitting to my wife that I've fallen once more. This coal I had seized long ago had yet to lose its destructive quality, and now it was not only I who was the victim of its fire but those closest to me. I had known since the first time I touched it that it was not a lawful thing for me to have. The shame which followed the pleasure told me this was true, but I had not the desire to let it go. Though it proved time and time again to be no good for me, I found its red-hot appearance too luring to forsake it. I saw no reason to abandon it until it became increasingly clear to me that, had I chosen to retain it, it would eventually set ablaze my entire life. This realization came by reason of the evidence of the figurative ash that surrounded me coupled with the knowledge of liberty that was lodged within my heart. I knew that, had I forsaken it, had I gotten rid of this my long-time companion, the fires would cease. But I also couldn't fathom life without the pleasure of its company. Through its tolerance of this unlawful thing, my heart, though it had known the knowledge of God, had forfeited the power of that knowledge, and so there I stood betwixt two ways: liberty and bondage.

Can a man take fire in his bosom and his clothes not be burned? Can one go upon hot coals, and his feet not be burned? ... But whoso committeth adultery with a woman lacketh understanding: he that doeth it destroyeth his own soul.

PROVERBS 6:27-28, 32

Solomon in the verses above is expressing the dangers of committing adultery, and he uses fire as a parallel to depict the destructive nature of such a sin. Jesus said that it is a sin for a man to even look upon a woman with the intent of lusting after her, so this text applies to all men. I, like many men, had chosen to handle the fire. I took it upon myself to touch the flames of sinful lust and, as I've stated, I reaped a degree of the consequences of having coddled the flame.

My marriage and my calling were the two greatest facets of my life that suffered the most damage. The fire had all but consumed the trust between my wife and me. The flames had burned their way into my conscience, creating in me a constant sense of ill preparedness with regard to preaching, teaching, and living the gospel of Jesus Christ which, as I understood, was my entire purpose in life. I was living in a constant state of misery for I knew what God was requiring of me, but I was not yet willing to let go. I was becoming what Paul referred to as a "castaway" in 1 Corinthians 9:27. Something had to give! I couldn't continue to stand idle in the way. I had to use the power God had given me and choose that path of liberty. I had to decide to either allow that flame that I had discovered long ago to continue to destroy my marriage, my calling, and my life or to simply put it down and leave it there.

So often as men, we discover things along the course of our lives that we find to be intensely captivating, and these discoveries often happen while in route to manhood. These discoveries don't just happen coincidentally though. Satan strategically places these enticements along our path. For me, it was the uncovering of a pornographic tape of my father's. Maybe it was something else for you. Whatever secret sin you may be harboring, I want you to begin to view it as a coal of fire no man can handle. It's important to view it as the destructive thing it is because Satan has already attempted to disguise it as something harmless and pleasing. You must not welcome this thing into your life any longer. It's time to put it down! It's time to release it from your possession and let it go!

I recently came across one of Aesop's fables, called *The Farmer and the Lion,* and I want to share it with you as I think it fitting for the topic at hand:

A lion entered one day into a farmyard, and the farmer, wishing to catch him, shut the gate. When the lion found that he could not get out, he began at once to attack the sheep and then the oxen. The farmer, afraid for himself, opened the gate, and the lion made off as fast as he could.

His wife, who had observed it all, when she saw her husband in great trouble at the loss of his cattle, cried out, "You are rightly served; for what could have made you so mad as to wish to detain a creature, whom, if you saw at a distance, you would wish further off?"

Better scare a thief than snare him.

In this short story, the farmer had a poor understanding of two things: the destructive nature of a lion and his natural inability to handle him. His lack of understanding is what lead to the destruction of his property and livelihood. He had no business catching, as his wife put it, "a creature, whom if you saw at a distance, you would wish further off." Going against reason, he attempted to snare the beast nonetheless, and we see how that turned out for him.

We too, like the farmer, have attempted to capture things we would have been better off leaving be. Whenever we pause to look upon a woman in a lustful manner, we're taking it upon ourselves to handle something well beyond what we are capable of managing. We must not allow the pleasures of sin to eclipse the destruction it will cause. Lust is an evil that, as the Bible says, "wars against the soul." This means that within us, within our flesh that is, there are carnal desires threatening to destroy us. But these desires that abide within our mortal bodies are not limited to those of a sexual nature only. We are capable of lusting after material possessions, money, power, popularity, alcohol, and anything else that appeals to our flesh.

As mane-bearers, we must always bear in mind that such

lusts threaten the appeal of our manes, which render us in-effective in honoring the Lord with our lives. We cannot be like the farmer in the short story who was void of the un-derstanding needed to avoid personal loss. When these fiery lusts arise in our hearts, we must quench the fire before it progresses into something we cannot handle. So, what's the point of all this? What's the bottom line?

DON'T WELCOME THE LION INTO YOUR HOUSE!

Many of us don't willingly invite Satan into our lives. We don't purpose to have him over for dinner and fellowship af-terward. It's never our intention for him to rule and there-by destroy our lives, but that's exactly what happens when we don't heed the Word of the Lord. Satan's intentions with us are to kill, to steal, and to ultimately destroy us and our prides. He's viciously roaming around the pride-lands of life, searching for men that are dull-minded like the farmer. He's looking for men who won't oppose his intrusion because they lack the understanding needed to see him as the killer he is. These men and their families are doomed for destruction un-less you and I possess the courage to call him out!

You and I can't be like the farmer. We must oppose his in-trusion with the attitude and grit of a lion that's dead serious about protecting his territory. There are men, families, and lineages depending on us to be obedient to the Lord. Their eternal futures are riding on us to put down the destructive and life-consuming coals in our lives and to choose, rather, to pick up our crosses and head in the direction of glory.

NOTES

And so it begins...

1. Vine, W. E., et al. *Vine's Expository Dictionary of Old & New Testament Words*, T. Nelson Publishers, Nashville, TN, 2003.

2. "Department of Defense Releases Fiscal Year 2020 Annual Report on Sexual Assault in the Mil." *U.S. Department of Defense*, https://www.defense.gov/News/Releases/Release/Article/2606508/department-of-defense-releases-fiscal-year-2020-annual-report-on-sexual-assault/.

3. "Department of Defense Releases Fiscal Year 2020 Annual Report on Sexual Assault in the Mil." *U.S. Department of Defense*, https://www.defense.gov/News/Releases/Release/Article/2606508/department-of-defense-releases-fiscal-year-2020-annual-report-on-sexual-assault/.

4. Orvis/ Director, Defense Suicide Prevention Office (DSPO), K. A. (2021). *Department of Defense (DoD) Quarterly Suicide Report (QSR) 3rd Quarter, CY 2021*. DSPO. https://www.dspo.mil/Portals/113/Documents/TAB%20A_20211230_OFR_Rpt_Q3_CY2021.pdf?ver=GDK03pwWqkz1-OLGo_qlxg%3d%3d

5. Orvis/ Director, Defense Suicide Prevention Office (DSPO), K. A. (2021). *Department of Defense (DoD) Quarterly Suicide Report (QSR) 3rd Quarter, CY 2021*. DSPO. https://www.dspo.mil/Portals/113/Documents/TAB%20A_20211230_OFR_Rpt_Q3_CY2021.pdf?ver=GDK03pwWqkz1-OLGo_qlxg%3d%3d

Chapter 1: The Way of the Mane

6. Packer, C. (2015). *Lions in the balance: Man-eaters, manes, and men with guns*. University of Chicago Press. Pages 7-8

7. Packer, C. (2015). *Lions in the balance: Man-eaters, manes, and men with guns*. University of Chicago Press. Page 28

Chapter 2: Selective Eater

8. George, J. (2015). *A Man After God's Own Heart*. Harvest House Publishers. Pages 24-25

Chapter 3: Men of Risk (MOR)

9. Piper, J. (2013). *Risk is right: Better to lose your life than to waste it*. Crossway. Page 10

10. Carr, S. (2021, April 27). *Robert Jermain Thomas – First protestant martyr in Korea*. Place For Truth. https://www.placefortruth.org/blog/robert-jermain-thomas-first-protestant-martyr-in-korea

Chapter 4: The Hopcraft Effect

11. HOPCRAFT, J. G., SINCLAIR, A. R., & PACKER, C. (2005). Planning for success: Serengeti lions seek prey accessibility rather than abundance. *Journal of Animal Ecology*, 74(3), 559-566. https://doi.org/10.1111/j.1365-2656.2005.00955.x

12. confluence. 2022. In *Merriam-Webster.com*.

Retrieved January 24, 2022, from https://www.merriam-webster.com/dictionary/confluence

Chapter 5: Teach Him to Reason

13. *Opinion: Imagining a world without lions*. (2013, August 6). National Geographic. https://www.nationalgeographic.com/adventure/article/130802-lions-extinction-opinion-animals-africa-joubert

14. Packer, C. (2015). *Lions in the balance: Man-eaters, manes, and men with guns*. University of Chicago Press. Page 141

15. strength. 2022. In *Merriam-Webster.com*. Retrieved February 5, 2022, from https://www.merriam-webster.com/dictionary/strength

Chapter 6: Territorial Trials

16. Farrar, S. (2009). *Point man: How a man can lead his family*. Multnomah. Page 43

17. Vine, W. E. (2003). *Vine's expository dictionary of the old and New Testament words*. Thomas Nelson. Page 583

18. Farrar, S. (2009). *Point man: How a man can lead his family*. Multnomah. Page 43

19. Vine, W. E. (2003). *Vine's expository dictionary of the old and New Testament words*. Thomas Nelson. Page 667

20. Packer, C. (2010, July 27). *Current Biology Volume 20 No 14*. https://www.cell.com/current-biology/pdf/S0960-9822%2810-%2900564-6.pdf. https://www.cell.com/current-biology/pdf/S0960-9822%2810%2900564-6.pdf

Chapter 7: Cleave to What is Good

21. Polly House. (2003, April 3). *Want your church to grow? Then bring in the men*. Baptist Press. https://www.baptistpress.com/resource-library/news/want-your-church-to-grow-then-bring-in-the-men/

22. Strong, J. (1996). *The new strong's exhaustive concordance of the Bible: Easy-to-read print, words of Christ emphasized, fan-tap thumb-index reference system, Greek and Hebrew dictionaries, strong's numbering system*. Thomas Nelson.

Chapter 8: The Mane Attraction

23. Guarino, B. (2017, December 12). *Women rate the strongest men as the most attractive, study finds*. The Washington Post. https://www.washingtonpost.com/news/speaking-of-science/wp/2017/12/12/women-rate-the-strongest-men-as-the-most-attractive-study-finds/

24. Guarino, B. (2017, December 12). *Women rate the strongest men as the most attractive, study finds*. The Washington Post. https://www.washingtonpost.com/news/speaking-of-science/

wp/2017/12/12/women-rate-the-strongest-men-as-the-most-attractive-study-finds/

25. Guarino, B. (2017, December 12). *Women rate the strongest men as the most attractive, study finds.* The Washington Post. https://www.washingtonpost.com/news/speaking-of-science/ wp/2017/12/12/women-rate-the-strongest-men-as-the-most-attractive-study-finds/

26. Guarino, B. (2017, December 12). *Women rate the strongest men as the most attractive, study finds.* The Washington Post. https://www.washingtonpost.com/news/speaking-of-science/ wp/2017/12/12/women-rate-the-strongest-men-as-the-most-attractive-study-finds/

27. Guarino, B. (2017, December 12). *Women rate the strongest men as the most attractive, study finds.* The Washington Post. https://www.washingtonpost.com/news/speaking-of-science/ wp/2017/12/12/women-rate-the-strongest-men-as-the-most-attractive-study-finds/

28. Guarino, B. (2017, December 12). *Women rate the strongest men as the most attractive, study finds.* The Washington Post. https://www.washingtonpost.com/news/speaking-of-science/ wp/2017/12/12/women-rate-the-strongest-men-as-the-most-attractive-study-finds/

Chapter 9: Apples to Apples

29. Statista Research Department. (2021, February 25). *Divorces - number in U.S. 2019 | Statista.* Statista. https://www.statista.com/ statistics/195939/number-of-divorces-in-the-united-states-since-1981/#statisticContainer

30. IFoster. (2020, November 9). *6 quick statistics on the current state of foster care – iFoster.* iFoster. https://www.ifoster.org/blogs/6-quick-statistics-on-the-current-state-of-foster-care/

31. Cherry, K. (2020, September 19). *How social comparison theory influences our views on ourselves.* Verywell Mind. Retrieved February 24, 2022, from https://www.verywellmind.com/what-is-the-social-comparison-process-2795872

Chapter 10: The Appeal of Passion

32. History.com Editors. (2009, November 4). *Vikings.* HISTORY. https://www.history.com/topics/exploration/vikings-history

33. History.com Editors. (2009, November 4). *Vikings.* HISTORY. https://www.history.com/topics/exploration/vikings-history

34. https://etvma.org/veterans/daniel-m-morris-12168/

Chapter 11: The Keystone of America

35. Denchak, M. (2019, September 9). *Keystone species 101.* NRDC. Retrieved February 28, 2022, from https://www.nrdc.org/stories/keystone-species-101

36. Roberts, S. (2016, June 17). *Robert Paine, ecologist who found 'Keystone species,' dies at 83 (Published 2016).* The New York Times - Breaking News, US News, World News and Videos. Retrieved February 28, 2022, from https://www.nytimes.com/2016/06/18/science/robert-paine-ecologist-who-found-keystone-species-dies-at-83.html

37. Carroll, S. B. (2016). *The Serengeti rules: The quest to discover how life works and why it matters.* Princeton University Press.

38. Blankenhorn, D. (1996). *Fatherless America: Confronting our most urgent social problem.* HarperCollins.

39. Prentzel, O. (2019, July 18). *Where lions once ruled, they are now quietly disappearing.* National Geographic. https://www.national-geographic.com/animals/article/lion-numbers-halved-since-original-lion-king#:~:text=With%20fewer%20than%20an%20estimated,the%20conservation%20status%20of%20species.&text=Lions%20were%20once%20found%20on,percent%20of%20their%20historic%20range

40. US Census Bureau. (2021, November). *Historical living arrangements of children.* Census.gov. Retrieved March 4, 2022, from https://www.census.gov/data/tables/time-series/demo/families/children.html